MEDITATION, MIND AND PATANJALI'S YOGA
A PRACTICAL GUIDE TO SPIRITUAL GROWTH FOR EVERYONE

Meditation, Mind & Patanjali's Yoga

A Practical Guide to Spiritual Growth for Everyone

by
Swami Bhaskarananda

Sri Ramakrishna Math
Mylapore, Chennai-4

Sri Ramakrishna Math
Mylapore, Chennai-600 004

Indian Edition © 2002 by Sri Ramakrishna Math, Chennai

Indian Printing and distrbution rights for this edition by special
permission of The Vedanta Society of Western Washington

First published in the United States: 2001
Meditation, Mind and Patanjali's Yoga
By Swami Bhaskarananda
© by The Vedanta Society of Western Washington

**III-3M 3C-2-2004
ISBN 81-7120-991-2**

Export of this book outside India is expressly prohibited.

Printed in India at
Sri Ramakrishna Math Printing Press
Mylapore, Chennai-4

*Dedicated to all those who are searching
for the Ultimate Truth*

Publisher's Note

We have great pleasure in presenting to our thoughtful readers this Indian edition of Swami Bhaskarananda's popular book on *Meditation, Mind and Patanjali's Yoga.*

Swami Bhaskarananda, a senior monk of the Ramakrishna Order, is the President of the Vedanta Society of Western Washington in Seattle USA. He is also the spiritual head of the Vedanta Society in Hawaii and of the Vedanta Society of Vancouver, Canada. He has travelled widely in both the East and West, spreading for three decades the Perennial Philosophy of Vedanta and enabling seekers to advance along their spiritual path.

After clearly explaining why we should meditate, the Swami underlines the need for a Guru. Then he details the eight steps that constitute Patanjali's system of Yoga. He takes care to point out the road-blocks in the path to the Supreme Goal and sheds much light on Kundalini Yoga, Samadhi and Mantra Japa. The fringe benefits of meditation in the form of stress-relief are also dwelt upon.

The book is, in short, a handbook for every one eager to realize the higher values of life and attain life's fulfilment. Read the book and discover how meditation restores to us the peace that is our birthright. We are thankful to the Vedanta Society of Western Washington for their gracious permission to bring out an Indian edition of their splendid book.

—Sri Ramakrishna Math, Chennai
August 2002

Table of Contents

List of Illustrations and Diagrams

Preface

For several years I have been frequently requested by our church members and friends to write a book on the techniques of controlling the mind with special emphasis on meditation. This book is a response to their request.

To write this book I have mainly relied on Patanjali's monumental work, the *Yoga-Sûtras*. Patanjali can be rightly called the first psychologist of ancient India. I have also taken help from other authentic books on Yoga and the personal experiences of renowned saints and sages. All efforts have been made to make the book as comprehensive as possible. A glance at its table of contents will convince the readers of my claim.

I have also tried to explain difficult and abstruse ideas with the help of stories and analogies in order to make the book easily understandable to the readers. Wherever needed, diagrams have been used. Also a special chapter dealing with how stress can be managed with the help of Yoga has been included in the book.

In the publication of this book the following persons have helped immensely and I acknowledge their loving assistance with deep gratitude.

- Swâmî Âtmatattwânanda of the Vedânta Society of Southern California for his help and assistance during the early stages of editing the book.
- Biswa Ranjan Chakraborty of Calcutta for providing two illustrations.
- Anadijiban Das for providing scientific information in regard to the interconvertablility of energy and matter.
- Richard Engstrom for designing and illustrating the cover.

- Allen R. Freedman for his assistance in proof-reading and preparing some of the diagrams.
- Devra A. Freedman for her help in editing and also preparing the glossary.
- Swamî Manishananda for his help in proofreading and for his suggestions.
- Charles Mathias for his many illustrations and assistance in preparing charts and diagrams.
- Swâmîs Mokshadânanda and Nishchalânanda—both of Belur Math, India—for their valuable suggestions.
- Master Nome of the Society of Abidance in Truth for permitting the use of Ramana Maharshi's photograph sent by him.
- Mithra Sankrithi for his help in proofreading and for his suggestions.
- Seattle Art Museum for permission to use the picture of a thirteenth century Chinese sculpture of a monk at the moment of his enlightenment.
- Stafford Smith for his assistance in proofreading and for his suggestions.
- Kathleen Teague for her help with some of the illustrations.
- Charles S. Wirth for providing assistance with the typesetting and printing of the manuscript.

I also thankfully acknowledge my debt to the following publisher.

- The Ramakrishna-Vivekananda Center of New York for permission to use quotations from *The Gospel of Sri Ramakrishna* and *Raja-Yoga* by Swamî Vivekananda.

I shall consider my labor well rewarded if the book proves to be helpful to the readers.

Swâmî Bhâskarânanda

Pronunciation Guide

Sanskrit and other Indian words have been carefully and consistantly transliterated—according to the chart below—hoping that the correct, or at least close, pronunciation will thus be indicated.

a is to be pronounced as in come

â is to be pronounced as in father

i is to be pronounced as in chili

î is to be pronounced as in machine

u is to be pronounced as in pull

û is to be pronounced as in intrude

ai is to be pronounced as in aisle

au is to be pronounced as in now

bh is to be pronounced as in abhor

ch is to be pronounced as in church

d is to be pronounced as thus

dh is to be pronounced as in adhere

g is to be pronounced as in god

gh is to be pronounced as in leghorn

kh is to be pronounced as in inkhorn

p is to be pronounced as in paternal

ph is to be pronounced as fine

th is to be pronounced as in thaw

sh is to be pronounced as in shall

INTRODUCTION

When all the senses are stilled, when the mind is at rest, when the intellect wavers not—then is known the highest state of Divinity.

The calm of the senses and the mind has been defined as Yoga. He who attains it is freed from delusion.

—*Katha Upanishad*

How to control the mind seems to have always been a great problem for most people. In the *Bhagavad Gîtâ*, an ancient scripture of Hinduism, Prince Arjuna laments to his friend and teacher Shrî Krishna, "O Krishna, my mind is naturally very restless. It constantly agitates my senses. It is extremely stubborn and resists all attempts to control it. It is just as difficult to control as it is to control the strong winds." Hindu tradition also compares an uncontrolled mind to a monkey which is totally drunk and is being stung by hornets. A naturally restless animal like a monkey becomes all the more restless when it is drunk and is being stung by hornets. This excellent analogy beautifully describes the pitiable state of an uncontrolled mind.

In this book I shall present some proven techniques of controlling the mind. These were developed by some ancient sages of India, among whom Patanjali is the most well-known. The practice of these techniques has helped innumerable people reach the acme of spiritual life—God realization. Along the way aspirants have also benefited from these techniques to gain success in their secular lives by mastering the art of concentration. Meditation is one of these techniques. But meditation and control of the mind are interdependent. They are complementary to each other. It is like riding a bicycle. To ride a bicycle one has to learn to pedal and steer at the same time. Only pedaling, or only steering, will not enable a person to ride a bike. Both have to be done simultaneously. Similarly, one has to initially exercise some control over one's mind to meditate. On the other hand, regular practice of meditation will eventually enable one to gain total control over one's mind.

Meditation, called *Dhyâna* in Sanskrit, has been used in India for several thousand years. The ascetics and Yogîs of India spent hundreds of years developing various meditation techniques. The Hindu sage Patanjali mastered the secrets of the human mind and wrote exhaustively about various meditation techniques in his famous book *Yoga-Sûtras,* or the *Aphorisms On Yoga.* Over the ages, those who have achieved spiritual illumination using these techniques have verified their efficacy.

During my more than forty years of ministry in India and North America I have come across many misconceptions about meditation. For instance, particularly in the West, some have the idea that chanting the holy name of God either silently or audibly is meditation. This, however, is not correct. This type of chanting is called Japa,[1] while meditation is called Dhyâna. Japa is one of the tech-

---

1. Please see Chapter XVII to know more about Japa.

niques to control the mind and have God vision. This book includes a large chapter on the techniques and benefits of Japa, side by side with several chapters dealing with the techniques and benefits of meditation.

It is not easy to meditate. Meditation is a state of intense concentration. Two analogies are often used to explain what Dhyâna or meditation is. In the first analogy, oil is being poured in an uninterrupted flow from a container into an empty bowl. Here oil symbolizes the mind and the bowl the object of thought. If the mind is made to flow in an uninterrupted manner to its object of thought for a prolonged period of time, it is called meditation.[2]

---

2. "Tatra pratyaikatânatâ dhyânam" i.e., "Uninterrupted thinking of one thought is Dhyâna or meditation."—*Yoga-Sûtras* 3/2.

The second analogy is that of an unflickering candle flame burning steadily in a windless place.[3] In this analogy the flame is the mind. The wind represents disturbance. The mind, free from disturbances, is in a state of meditation; it is engaged in one-pointed thinking only. The object of this one-pointed thinking, however, has to be holy. If it is secular or unholy it cannot be called meditation. This point will be discussed in greater detail in the succeeding chapters.

Lastly, I would like to point out here that the practice of meditation can benefit everyone irrespective of one's religious affiliation. It can even help an atheist find the ultimate Truth.

---

3. "Yathâ dîpo nivâtastho nengate sopamâ smritâ," i.e., "As a lamp in a windless spot does not flicker."—*Bhagavad Gîtâ* 6/19.

I

WHY WE SHOULD MEDITATE

Over the years many people have come and said to me, "Swâmî, I don't have any power of concentration." But there is no valid basis for such thinking. Everyone, even a child, can concentrate. While watching cartoons on TV, children display great concentration. At that time their minds appear to be glued to the TV screen.

It is not true that we cannot concentrate. What we lack is the ability to concentrate our minds on everything, and under all circumstances. It is easy to concentrate on what is pleasant. The difficulty arises when we have to concentrate on something unpleasant. A student finds it hard to concentrate on a dull and uninteresting book, and a parishioner feels drowsy when listening to a boring sermon.

Yet, all that is pleasant is not necessarily good. On the other hand, what is unpleasant may be good and beneficial. We must learn to concentrate on whatever we do, whether pleasant or unpleasant, as long as it is beneficial for us. Meditation—which is no other than training in concentration—can enable us to do this.

Concentration is indispensable in achieving success in life. Success in no area of human life can be attained without it. Swâmî Vivekânanda (1863-1902) used to say that

Swâmî Vivekânanda
(1863-1902)

the difference between a genius and an idiot is in their powers of concentration.[1]

Some say that meditation is good for health. It removes stress by relaxing the body and mind. It reduces high blood pressure. It helps slow down the aging process and improves memory. Some also say that meditation helps in gaining supernatural powers. While these claims may be true, the sages tell us that these are not the best reasons to meditate. Rather, meditation has a much higher purpose.

The highest goal of meditation is God-Realization or experiencing the Ultimate Truth

According to the sages, we should meditate in order to achieve the highest goal of human life—experiencing Divinity or the Ultimate Truth. It should be clearly understood that meditation or Dhyâna is only a means. It is not the goal itself. The most mature form of meditation is Samâdhi. In Samâdhi the mind becomes free from all

---

1. Born in Calcutta, India, as Narendranath Datta, Swâmî Vivekânanda lived for only 39 years. Yet he is considered one of the greatest saints of modern India and a national hero. He was the foremost disciple of Shrî Râmakrishna Paramahamsa, the renowned 19th century saint of India. The Swâmî's birthday, named National Youth Day by the Government of India, has been declared a national holiday. He attended the historic Parliament of Religions held in Chicago in 1893 as a delegate of Hinduism. A man of extraordinary scholarship and great oratorical skill, he turned out to be the star performer at the Parliament. It was he who first effectively preached Hinduism in Europe and North America. He founded a monastic organization named the Râmakrishna Order, the branches of which render humanitarian and religious services all over the world.

thoughts and is absolutely still. Patanjali calls this state of mind Yoga.[2] Even Samâdhi is only a means to an end.[3]

Samâdhi has been described as the super-conscious state of the mind. In that super-conscious state a spiritual aspirant goes beyond the domain of matter, and experiences the inherent Divine Spirit. Swâmî Vivekânanda has beautifully explained this in his monumental work *Râja Yoga:*

> When I eat food I do it consciously, when I assimilate it I do it unconsciously; when the food is manufactured into blood, it is done unconsciously; when out of the blood all the different parts of my body are strengthened, it is done unconsciously. And yet it is I who am doing all this; there cannot be twenty people in this one body. How do I know that I do it, and nobody else? It may be urged that my business is only to eat and assimilate the food, and that somebody else does the strengthening of the body by the food for me. That cannot be; because it can be demonstrated that almost every action of which we are now unconscious can be brought up to the plane of consciousness. The heart is beating apparently without our control; none of us can control the heart; it goes on its own way. But by practice men can bring even the heart under con-

---

2. In the West, Yoga is often incorrectly known to be only some physical postures that can enhance health and longevity. In India—where all these techniques were originally developed—such exercises are called Hatha Yoga. The word *Yoga* has many other meanings. In the context of spiritual life it means methods which help one in establishing communion with the Divine Reality, viz. Râja Yoga, Jnâna Yoga, Bhakti Yoga, Karma Yoga, etc.

3. To know more about Samâdhi see Chapter XV.

trol, until it will just beat at will, slowly or quickly, or almost stop. Nearly every part of the body can be brought under control. What does this show? It shows that we also perform the functions, which are beneath consciousness, only we are performing them unconsciously. We have, then, two planes in which the human mind works. First is the conscious plane, in which all work is always accompanied by the feeling of "I." Next comes the unconscious plane, where the work is unaccompanied by the feeling of "I." That part of the mind's work which is unaccompanied by egoism is unconscious work, and that part which is accompanied by egoism is conscious work. In the lower animals this unconscious work is called instinct. In higher animals, and in the highest of all animals, man, what is called conscious work prevails.

But the matter does not end here. There is a still higher plane on which the mind can work. It can go beyond consciousness. Just as unconscious work is beneath consciousness, so there is another sort of work that is above consciousness and that also is not accompanied by egoism. The feeling of "I" is only on the middle plane. When the mind is above or below that plane, there is no feeling of "I," and yet the mind works. When the mind goes beyond the plane of self-consciousness, it experiences Samâdhi, or superconsciousness. But how do we know that a man in Samâdhi has not gone below consciousness, has not degenerated instead of going higher? In both cases the experience is unaccompanied by the feeling of "I." The answer is that by the effects, by the results of the work, we know which is below, and which is above. When a man goes into deep sleep he enters a plane beneath consciousness. His body functions all the time; he breathes, perhaps he moves the body in his sleep, without any accompanying feeling of "I"; he is unconscious, and when he returns from his sleep he is the same man who went into it. The sum total of the knowledge that he had before he went to sleep remains the same; it does not increase at all. No enlightenment comes. But when a man goes into Samâdhi, if he goes into it a fool, he comes out a sage.... As this illumination with which a man comes back from Samâdhi is much higher than can be got from unconsciousness, or much higher than can be got by reasoning in a conscious state, it must therefore be superconsciousness, and so Samâdhi is called the superconscious state. This in short, is the idea of Samâdhi.[4]

All theistic religions believe in the omnipresence of God. Among them Hinduism most emphatically speaks of the presence of Divinity in every human being. At any given point in time Divinity is equally present in all, but not equally manifest. The purpose of all spiritual practices, including meditation, is to fully manifest this inherent Divinity. Only in the state of Samâdhi or Yoga does this Divinity become fully manifest. Then a person is said to have become a God-realized soul.

This Divinity is our true Self. It forms the very core of our being. We can give up whatever is extraneous, but not that which forms the very core of our existence. Sooner or later this true Self, this Divinity, must manifest itself. All

4. Swâmî Vivekânanda, *Râja Yoga* (New York: Râmakrishna-Vivekânanda Center, 1982), 75-77.

without exception will eventually experience this Divine Self manifested in them in Its infinite splendor. This is God-realization. This is the inevitable goal of human life.

Hinduism teaches that Infinite Bliss is one of the principal aspects of Divinity. We all yearn to have joy. This longing is expressed through our craving for money, sense pleasure, name, fame, power and position. Through all these cravings we are unconsciously trying to reach our Divine Self—Infinite Bliss. No matter how much pleasure, money, power or fame we have, we are never satisfied. We yearn for more. Finding lasting satisfaction through them is impossible, because the joy derived from them is finite. Only Infinite Joy can satisfy us. Eventually we realize that searching for Infinite Joy through finite and external means will lead us nowhere.

This realization will inspire us to turn around and consciously search for that fountain of Infinite Bliss within. When we arrive at this perennial source of Bliss all our wants and cravings will disappear forever. We will then experience God, the all-pervading Divinity, as Supreme Bliss both within ourselves and without—in everything that exists in this entire interminable universe. We will experience God as the essence of every thing and every being. We will love all—even our enemies—because we will see no enemy anywhere. In this state, any interaction with the world will be a most joyous and rewarding experience, because it is no other than directly interacting with God. We will see ourselves joyfully involved in a Divine play where God is playing all the roles, including our own. We will no longer identify with our body-mind-complexes, which are subject to birth, change, decay and death.[5] We will gain the unshakable conviction that we are the eternal Divine Spirit—deathless and birthless. Thus we will transcend all fear, suffering and sorrow. The *Bhagavad Gîtâ*, a well-known scripture of Hinduism, says: "After gaining that experience one thinks that there is no greater gain than that experience, and being established in that experience one is not moved even by the heaviest of sorrows."[6]

Buddhism and Jainism also use various time-honored techniques of meditation. Their spiritual goal is to go beyond all types of suffering. Yoga—the most mature state of meditation—helps one to reach that goal.

Methods of God-realization— the four Yogas

Besides what has been mentioned above, the Sanskrit word *Yoga* also means a yoke or a link—a link between the spiritual aspirant and God. In addition, the word *Yoga* has another technical meaning. It means a technique or path by following which we can establish communion with God.

---

5. Man is a combination of (1) the physical body, (2) the vital energy, (3) the sense organs, (4) the motor organs and (5) the mind. These put together are called the body-mind-complex. Although involved with the body-mind-complex, the soul of man is not a part of it. The soul is eternal, changeless, infinite, and the only source of consciousness. Man's body-mind-complex acquires consciousness by borrowing it from the soul. The soul is also called the Divine Spirit, the Divine Self, and the Divine Essence.
6. "Yam labdhvâ châparam lâbham manyate nâdhikam tatah. Yasmin sthito na duhkhena gurunâpi vichâlyate."—*Bhagavad Gîtâ* 6/22.

Hinduism offers many different Yogas or techniques to reach God. Out of them four are most important as they correspond to the four broad catagories into which Hinduism classes all spiritual seekers. These Yogas are:

(1) Bhakti Yoga or the path of devotion. This path is meant primarily for people who are temperamentally emotional and respond easily to love and affection.

(2) Jnâna Yoga or the path of rational inquiry. This path is prescribed for people of rational temperament to whom reason appeals more than faith.

(3) Râja Yoga or the path of psychic control. Raja Yoga is for aspirants who are of meditative temperament with a natural yearning to completely master their minds.

(4) Karma Yoga or the path of right action. The path of Karma Yoga is most attractive to people who are habitually very active.

All these paths, except for Karma Yoga, prescribe their own kinds of meditation to experience Divinity. (The path of Karma Yoga teaches the practice of selfless action as a means to experience Divinity. It does not teach meditation.) Râja Yoga, however, puts maximum emphasis on meditation. This book will discuss the techniques of concentration offered by the above mentioned three Yogas, but it will dwell more on those prescribed by Râja Yoga.

II

TEACHER AND STUDENT RELATIONSHIP

Why we need a teacher

People in the West often ask whether they need a teacher to learn how to meditate. The answer is a definite "Yes." By reading a book on meditation we can surely learn how to do simple meditation, but personal guidance from a competent teacher is far better. Students will encounter difficulties—even hazards—while practicing meditation. Owing to lack of experience they may not be able to handle these problems without the help of a competent teacher. The type of meditation they pick up from books may not be suitable for them and could slow their progress, or even harm them.

No two persons are alike; everyone is unique. And every person requires spiritual practices tailored to suit himself or herself. An experienced teacher is better able to wisely judge which spiritual practices will be suitable for a student. For this reason, religions such as Hinduism, Jainism, Buddhism and Sufism consider a spiritual teacher an absolute necessity.

In these traditions, the relationship between the spiritual teacher and the student is based on mutual faith and trust. The student must have faith in the teacher; otherwise the student won't feel the urge to follow the teacher's instructions. And the teacher should also have faith in the student. The teacher's faith in the student will greatly enhance the student's yearning to learn.

A true spiritual teacher must never charge money for giving spiritual instruction. Hindu, Buddhist, and Jain traditions strongly forbid it. But the teacher may accept gifts given by students out of gratitude.

The difficulty of finding a competent teacher and avoiding spurious ones

Unfortunately, there are far too many spurious teachers in the world. Finding a proper teacher of meditation, or for that matter any spiritual teacher, is difficult—but not impossible. As long as there is a demand for true teachers, numerous false teachers will abound. As long as good money is in demand, lots of counterfeit money will be in circulation. A realistic view of this world reveals that proportionately what is best is always the least. There is very little cream in milk, very little perfume in flowers, and only a small number of good and noble people in the world. The same applies to genuine spiritual teachers. Their number is negligible compared to the relatively large number of fake teachers. With no quality control inspectors in religion, false teachers continue to exploit the ignorant and gullible without hindrance.

Exploitation is a chronic illness in human society. A study of world history reveals that the powerful and unscrupulous have always exploited the less powerful. Those with stronger muscles have exploited the weak. The wealthy have used the poor. The more intelligent have abused the less intelligent. Militarily powerful nations have exploited weaker nations.. We needn't, therefore, be surprised that so many false spiritual teachers and charlatans take advantage of the unsuspecting and gullible.

False spiritual teachers exist in all countries and races. Many people become victims of pseudo-spiritual teachers. In my youth I was once a victim of a questionable teacher. From my own experience and that of others, I can attest that the methods employed by these spurious teachers are extremely clever and deceptive. They use just about every means of deception to entrap their victims and exploit them. At this point serious spiritual seekers must ask, "How can we protect ourselves from fake teachers and find one who is genuine?" My answer is that we should use our God-given intelligence to protect ourselves from questionable teachers. Hindu scriptures such as the *Katha Upanishad* (I/2/5) and the *Mundaka Upanishad* (I/2/8) advise spiritual aspirants to be intelligent and "not behave like the blind led by the blind." Shrî Râmakrishna (1836-1886), the well-known 19th century saint of India, used to say, "Be a good devotee of God, but don't be a fool."

To be ignorant and gullible is neither a great spiritual quality nor a commendable worldly virtue. Yet there are so many gullible people in the world. Phineas T. Barnum, of the well-known Barnum & Bailey Circus of America, is said to have once remarked, "There's a sucker born every minute." These words are just as true today as they were one hundred years ago.

Lately, fake spiritual teachers have begun using highly sophisticated multimedia propaganda techniques. They skillfully use publicity to influence and entrap people. Joseph Goebbels, the infamous head of the propaganda

Shrî Râmakrishna
(1836-1886)

department in Hitler's Germany, reportedly said, "If you tell a lie one hundred times it becomes the truth." Genuine spiritual seekers must be extremely cautious and not fall into such traps.

People often use the wrong criteria to judge spiritual teachers. Once a gentleman came to me and said, "I'm lucky to be the disciple of a great saint. My teacher at one time was a well-known Harvard professor." It sounded rather odd. Spiritual teachers ought to be judged by their present spiritual qualities, not by their past worldly achievements. Success in secular life, whether in the past or present, is not the right criterion to judge the spirituality of a teacher.

There are some questionable spiritual teachers whose tactics include flattering the egos of those who come to them. I knew one teacher who would flatter the egos of his potential followers by telling them that they had been very famous people in their past lives. He told one middle-aged lady that she was Michelangelo[1] in her previous incarnation. This made her feel important.

Some people are like moths. They want to jump into fire and die. They would rather be swindled and cheated by charlatans than use their God-given intelligence! No words of caution can dissuade them. True spiritual seekers are expected to behave differently. They are expected to be rational and capable of making sound judgments. Some guidelines are given below to help inexperienced spiritual seekers differentiate genuine saints and teachers from spurious ones.

---

1. Michelangelo Buonarroti (1475-1564), famous Italian painter and sculptor.

Characteristics of genuine spiritual teachers

(1) Genuine spiritual teachers have no ulterior selfish motives. They always think of the spiritual and mundane well-being of others.

(2) They do not crave praise, honor or fame. If praised by others they feel embarrassed. Yet they are always eager to give praise and honor to others.

(3) They are beyond lust and greed. Both lust and greed are rooted in selfishness. Genuine spiritual teachers are totally unselfish.

(4) They do not crave money. The scriptures of Hinduism say that one cannot have eternal life unless one has renounced wealth and the craving for progeny.[2] The New Testament says, "No man can serve two masters...Ye cannot serve God and mammon [together]."[3]

Why do these scriptures consider money an impediment to spiritual life? Money is nothing but potential sense enjoyment. In exchange for money we get objects of sense enjoyment. Attachment to money is no other than attachment to sense pleasure. Tulasi Das, a well-known saint of India, used to say, "God isn't there where there is desire for sense pleasure. Where God is, there is no desire for sense pleasure."[4] As spiritually illumined teachers are not attached to sense pleasure, they are not attached to money either.

---

2. "Na karmanâ na prajayâ dhanena tyâgenaike amritattwamâ-nasu"—"Not by work, progeny or wealth, but by renunciation alone immortality can be achieved."—*Kaivalya Upanishad*, 3.
3. The Gospel according to St. Matthew 6:24.
4. The saying in Hindi is—"Jahân kâm tahân nahi Râm, jahân Râm tahân kâm nahi."

Once, somewhere in India, a holy man was sitting in his Ashrama (monastery) in the presence of his disciples. A wealthy disciple of the holy man came, laid a package at the feet of his Guru, and saluted him.

"What's this package for?" asked the holy man.

The disciple replied, "This is a small gift for you, sir. It contains one hundred thousand rupees."[5]

As soon as he heard this comment the holy man kicked the package away. The disciple felt very humiliated and said to his Guru, "Revered sir, you won't find too many disciples who can give you one hundred thousand rupees!"

The holy man said, "And you won't find too many Gurus either who can kick away one hundred thousand rupees!"

Genuine spiritual teachers never charge money for giving spiritual instructions. To impress people, spurious spiritual teachers of independent means also may not take money from their students. Nevertheless, they crave honor, adoration and appreciation from their students.

(5) Genuine spiritual teachers do not look upon themselves as either teachers or saints. Their natural humility prevents them from doing so. They feel embarrassed when others call them saints or teachers. They give their teachings without the vanity of a teacher.

(6) They never write books or autobiographies to glorify themselves; nor do they indulge in any other kind of self-

---

5. The rupee is the standard currency in India—like the dollar in the United States.

Keshab Chandra Sen
(1838–1884)

aggrandizement. If they write books at all, they do so as a service to mankind or God. As long as they are alive, they are against anyone writing their biographies.

(7) They are not interested in any kind of publicity. One such example is Shrî Râmakrishna. Among his many admirers was Brahmânanda Keshab Chandra Sen, the renowned leader of the reformist Brâhmo Samâj Church of India. Impressed by Shrî Râmakrishna's saintliness, Keshab Chandra Sen wrote an article in his church journal, *The Indian Mirror,* appreciating the saint. Hearing of this, Shrî Râmakrishna felt extremely embarrassed. When Keshab Chandra Sen came to see him, Shrî Râmakrishna said, "Keshab, why did you write about me? You needn't publicize me! If God so wills, He will decide whether people should know about me or not."

(8) Genuine spiritual teachers may start organizations but will never name them after themselves. Nor will they allow an organization founded by their admirers to be named after them. They may found organizations and out of reverence and gratitude name them after their deceased Gurus or spiritual teachers. Swâmî Vivekânanda, for example, founded the Râmakrishna Mission, the well-known philanthropic organization in India. He named it after his deceased Guru, Shrî Râmakrishna—not after himself.

(9) Truthfulness is one of the most important qualities of genuine spiritual teachers. If they lie they are not fit to be teachers.

(10) Genuine spiritual teachers practice what they preach. They do not advise others to do what they themselves would not do.

Shrî Chaitanya
(1485–1533)

Once a poor widow came with her young son to see a holy man. The boy was extremely fond of candy. Due to her poverty, it was very hard for the woman to buy candy for her son. She said to the holy man, "Sir, will you kindly ask my son not to eat candy? I have asked him many times, but my words haven't produced any effect. You are a holy man; I'm sure he will listen to your advice."

Thereupon, the holy man said to her, "Please bring your son back in seven days. I'll talk to him then."

They returned in seven days, but the holy man asked them to come back again after another week. When they came back the second time, the holy man said to her son, "My child, don't eat candies; they're not good for you!"

The mother said, "Sir, why didn't you say this to him the very first day we came to see you?"

The holy man replied, "I myself was fond of eating candy. I didn't have the right then to ask your son to give up eating candy. It has taken me two weeks to get over this weakness. Now I've gained the right to ask him not to eat candy."

(11) Genuine spiritual teachers are not mystery-mongers. They do not mystify religion. They do not want to awe people by claiming to have miraculous powers, nor do they ordinarily want to display them. If at all they perform miracles under the inspiration of God, they consider that to be God's glory, not their own.

(12) They are never depressed or morose. They are always peaceful and cheerful. They are humorous, but their humor does not hurt or ridicule anyone; they use it to help people spiritually.

(13) They are naturally nonviolent, kind, and considerate. They never become really angry. Sometimes they may make a show of mock anger to discipline their students for their spiritual good.

(14) Humility is a special distinguishing quality of all genuine spiritual teachers and saints. All great spiritual teachers and saints are humble.

In India there lived a monk in the holy city of Vrindaban. The monk fell from grace having had an immoral relationship with a woman. As a result, other monks in the city shunned him.

One day, all the monks of Vrindaban were invited to a feast given by a very wealthy person. Along with other monks, the fallen monk also went to the wealthy man's home for the feast. This caused a commotion in the dining hall. The assembled monks said to the host, "None of us will sit and eat here unless you ask the fallen monk to leave."

The most famous Vaishnava saint of Vrindaban was also present among the assembled monks. The saint was renowned for his humility and other saintly qualities. Ignoring what the other monks had been demanding he took his seat in the dining hall and made the fallen monk sit next to him. Then he said to the other monks, "Brothers, I consider this monk to be my Guru. By his own life's example he has taught me what humiliation and misfortune one has to go through when fallen from grace."

The saint's humility touched the hearts of the monks. They all then quietly sat down to eat.

Shrî Sâradâ Devî
(1853–1920)

Shrî Chaitanya (1485-1533), a great spiritual teacher and saint of India, said in one of his teachings, "A true lover of God is humbler than even a blade of grass, and more enduring than a tree. He craves neither respect nor honor. Yet he is always willing to give honor and respect to others." A tree, when being cut down by a logger, silently endures the pain. Nevertheless, it does not deprive the logger of its fruits or shade. So also a true lover of God withstands all sufferings inflicted on him or her by others and yet does not stop serving them.

Why are genuine saints humble? How do they acquire humility? According to our scriptures, a saint's humility is the outcome of many years of intense spiritual practice. Simply making a New Year's resolution such as, "From today onwards I shall be humble," is not likely to make anyone humble! Only after many years of steadfast spiritual practice can true humility be gained.

When engaging in spiritual practice one has to eliminate both external and internal defects. It is relatively easier to eliminate external defects, but very hard to get rid of internal ones, which lie hidden in the deeper layers of the mind and have yet to be discovered. Once discovered, repeated attempts must be made to eliminate them. These defects are much more subtle than external ones. Craving for name and fame and yearning for attention and praise are two examples of subtle internal defects. Sârada Devî, a great 19th century woman saint of India, used to say that external defects are like so many knots in a thick rope; it is comparatively easy to untie them. The subtler internal defects are like knots in a thin hair; undoing them is extremely difficult.

As mentioned earlier, one cannot overcome defects by trying only once. Repeated attempts have to be made. As success comes only after many failed attempts, one develops humility, and cannot feel superior to others.

Lately the expression *self-esteem* has gained considerable popularity. We are asked to get rid of our low self-esteem in order to succeed in life. Some believers in self-esteem consider humility harmful. According to them, humility is lack of self-esteem. This view, however, is not correct. Humility is a realistic recognition of our imperfections. It does not make us feel worthless; it urges us to strive for perfection.

According to some psychologists the motivation for gaining superiority comes from a sense of inferiority. Recognition of our imperfections does not necessarily mean that we lack self-esteem. When we see our imperfections and think that we can never improve, only then are we lacking in self-esteem—otherwise not. If a sense of inferiority urges us to succeed in spiritual or mundane life by ridding ourselves of our imperfections, then we surely are not suffering from any lack of self-esteem. On the contrary, we are in the process of healthy psychological growth.

(15) In addition to all these qualities, a genuine spiritual teacher should also have a good spiritual lineage. A teacher must be a student of a genuine saint of proven reliability. Even to acquire secular knowledge, it is wise to go to teachers with good academic backgrounds. These teachers are reliable. Similarly, it is safer to go to a spiritual teacher with a good spiritual lineage.

The reliability of a spiritual teacher is usually proven with the passage of time. There is a saying, "Time is the best healer." In a special sense time is also the best "killer." Imposters claiming to be great saints may fool some gullible people during their lifetimes, but in time people discover their deceptions. Time eventually "kills" their so-called saintly images. Abraham Lincoln once rightly said, "It is true that you may fool all the people some of the time; you can even fool some of the people all of the time; but you can't fool all of the people all of the time."[6] Thus, a spiritual seeker must carefully avoid a self-proclaimed saint or teacher who lacks a proper spiritual lineage.

Some tactics of fake spiritual teachers

As mentioned earlier, once I myself was the victim of a fake spiritual teacher. I know how these teachers use various kinds of deception in their clandestine trade of exploitation. Below are some of the techniques they use to swindle people:

(1) Fake teachers usually try to project a mysterious image. This is often achieved by making themselves less accessible. A teacher whom I knew used to lock himself in his bedroom for the major part of the day. Nobody could see him at that time. He would also occasionally take a vow of silence and communicate by whispering or writing on a slate. Only for an hour or two in the morning and for two hours in the evening would he come out of his room to meet people. His admirers would imagine that during all those hours inside his room he was immersed in Samâdhi (a state of communion with God)! The room where he

---

6. Quoted from Alexander McClure's *Lincoln's Yarns and Stories*.

met people in the evening would be kept poorly lit, to create a mysterious atmosphere. It had electric lights, but they would not be turned on. A single candle would be burning, creating more shadows than light.

Another tactic used by false teachers is to maintain several secretaries. To talk to them you have to go through these secretaries. If you want an interview with such a teacher you will not get it immediately. You have to wait. Unless you are a celebrity or very wealthy you will be made to wait for days—even months. In this manner the teachers enhance their image by making themselves inaccessible. Easy availability would make them less important.

(2) I know of one questionable teacher who claims to have acquired some ancient and secret techniques from a mysterious holy man. He also claims that he alone has been empowered to teach those secret techniques to certain chosen people, preferably the rich and the famous.

(3) People have a natural reluctance to work hard. The owner of a door-to-door fruit delivery business in the Seattle area wanted to hire some college students to sell fruits door-to-door during the summer months. He placed the following ad in a local daily newspaper:

"Sales—Temporary Summer Employment. Work Hard. Earn Good Money."

The ad ran for 7 days, and there was not even a single response. The owner then put the following modified ad in the newspaper for another 7 days :

"Sales—Temporary Summer Employment. Have Fun In The Sun. Earn Good Money."

The ad brought 134 phone responses in one week. After hearing the job description ten agreed to show up that Saturday morning at 9 AM for work. Of that ten, five actually showed up. Of that five, only one was a hard worker. During that summer three of the five young men were caught stealing money. They had to be fired.

The same is true for spiritual life. Few are willing to work hard to achieve spiritual progress. Taking advantage of that reluctance, some fake teachers claim that hard work will not be necessary for those who become their students. They also claim that by their spiritual powers they can awaken the students' dormant spirituality and liberate them here and now. Such claims are utterly false. The food in our stomach cannot be digested by anyone else. So also with spiritual progress—it is we who have to work hard for it; no one else can do it for us.

A teacher can only give us guidance and inspiration. We must follow our teacher's guidance and work hard to progress spiritually. The expression *spiritual practice* means repetitive spiritual effort. Intense spiritual effort has to be made over and over again to achieve the goal of spiritual life. "Success is speedy for the extremely energetic," says Patanjali.[7]

(4) One technique that false teachers use is to flatter the egos of their students. I knew a teacher in India who used to tell his students that they had been highly advanced souls in their previous incarnations and were born this time to assist him in propagating his message throughout the entire world, preferably in the affluent West. Another

---

7. "Tîvra-samvegânâm-âsannah"—*Yoga-Sûtras*, 1/21.

questionable teacher visiting Canada from India tried to encourage a bright young man of East Indian ancestry—who was doing his postgraduate work in the University of Toronto—to come along with him to India and become his monastic disciple. He said to the young man, "If you become my disciple, I promise I'll send you later to the United States as the head of my Ashrama in Hawaii."

No ordinary mortal can become a Guru or teacher overnight. According to Hindu tradition, God is the only true spiritual teacher. Out of compassion for mankind God incarnates on earth for the salvation of His creatures. Divine Incarnations, being ever perfect, are the true teachers of mankind. No one other than a Divine Incarnation can become a spiritual teacher or Guru overnight. Those who have experienced God after years of intense spiritual practice may be able to play the role of a teacher only after having been commissioned by God. They teach, but without the vanity of a teacher. They consider themselves to be instruments in the hands of God. There is no instant success in spiritual life. For some spiritual aspirants God-realization may not even come during one lifetime! Yet, everyone wants to be a Guru!

Once a young man came to the abbot of a monastery and said, "Sir, I want to become a monk. Please permit me to join the monastery."

The abbot said, "If you want to be a monk you should be prepared to do a lot of hard work. Every day you must get up from bed two hours before sunrise. After having a shower you have to mop the temple floor, help cook all the meals for the monks, do the dishes, take care of the vegetable garden, draw water from the stream to water the plants, take care of the guests, clean the cowshed, and mow the lawns. And over and above all this, you have to regularly study the scriptures, and meditate three times a day."

The young man said, "I've understood what a newly admitted monk has to do. But, sir, may I ask what an abbot is expected to do?"

The abbot replied, "Well, not much. He has to perform the duties of a Guru, such as giving spiritual instruction to his disciples, talking to visitors, and instructing the monks about their day-to-day duties."

Thereupon, the young man said, "In that case, sir, please make me a Guru. I think that position will suit me best!"

(5) Another technique fake teachers may use is to pretend to be all-knowing. With the help of accomplices they first collect information about the unsuspecting people who visit them. Using that information, they try to create the false impression that they know everything about them.

(6) False teachers may start religious communes and encourage their followers to come and live with them. Those joining these communes are almost totally controlled by these teachers. A lady whom I knew became a resident of a certain religious commune on the East Coast of the United States. After a few years she became disillusioned with her teacher and decided to leave. But she was not allowed to leave. Other members of the commune watched her constantly. Finally, in the dead of night she somehow managed to escape. Walking many miles on foot she was able to reach the nearest railroad station and eventually go to her parents in California. After her escape

she wrote to me giving all the details of her unfortunate experience at the commune. She wrote that she had to give them all her money when she joined and was not allowed to have contact with anyone other than the members of the commune. She was not allowed to communicate with relatives or friends, or even her parents.

What happens when a sincere spiritual seeker becomes a victim of a false teacher?

Most people's spiritual journey starts with a craving for miracles and mysteries. This is the stage of the mystery-monger. A mystery is something unknown. Once we know it, it has ceased to be a mystery. The same is true for miracles. To us, TV and airplanes are not miracles. But to people out of touch with modern civilization—these would be miracles. In this mystering-mongering stage we are most vulnerable to exploitation by crooks and charlatans, and no matter how sincere we are, we are more prone to fall into the traps of deceitful teachers. To grow spiritually we must go beyond the mystery-mongering stage.

If sincere and trusting people fall into the trap of a deceitful teacher, what will happen to them? Will everything be lost? Hindu tradition says that such aspirants, in spite of having an incompetent teacher, may make some spiritual progress—provided they have genuine faith in God. A false teacher is like a dirty broom. Though dirty itself, it can still clean a dirty floor, even though not perfectly. Sooner or later sincere students will discover the true color of their teacher. Their disillusionment will then protect them like a powerful vaccine from other questionable teachers. After this experience they are more likely to know who a genuine spiritual teacher is.

Shraddhâ—a necessary ingredient of student life

Religions such as Hinduism, Jainism, Judaism, Buddhism, and Sufism traditionally accord great honor and respect to spiritual teachers. "Treat your teacher as a god," says the sacred text of the *Taittiriya Upanishad*.[8] Hinduism maintains that spiritual knowledge can only be acquired by students with Shraddhâ for their teacher.[9] Shraddhâ is a Sanskrit word without an exact counterpart in English. Shraddhâ means respect, implicit faith, and trust. It also means self-confidence. Besides having the greatest respect for our teachers, we must have implicit faith and trust in them. We must also have the self-confidence that we will surely be able to experience God with our teachers' help, even though the path of spiritual progress, as the scriptures say, has many obstacles and difficulties.[10]

On the other hand, teachers must also have confidence in their students. This confidence in the students will help generate the students' self-confidence.

---

8. "Âchâryadevo Bhava"—*Taittiriya Upanishad* I/11/2.
9. "Shraddhâvân labhate jnânam"—"One who has Shraddhâ acquires knowledge."—*Bhagavad Gîtâ*, 4/39.
10. "Kshurasya dhârâ nishitâ duratyayâ durgam pathastat kavayo vadanti," i.e. "The wise describe that [spiritual] path to be as inaccessible as a razor's sharp edge, which is difficult to tread on."—*Katha Upanishad*, I/3/14.

III

STEPS TO YOGA
The Acme Of Meditation

After finding a competent teacher, students have to go step by step through a course designed to help them master meditation. Patanjali prescribes the following eight-step discipline to attain this goal. As mentioned earlier, this goal is also called Yoga.

Patanjali's eight-step discipline to Yoga

1. Yama: Restraining harmful thoughts and impulses.
2. Niyama: Cultivating good habits.
3. Âsana: Learning sitting postures suitable for prolonged contemplation.
4. Prânâyâma: Learning the technique of rhythmic breathing.
5. Pratyâhâra: Withdrawing the senses from their objects of enjoyment.
6. Dhâranâ: Fixing the mind on the object of contemplation.
7. Dhyâna: Uninterrupted contemplation, also called meditation.
8. Samâdhi: Total absorption of the mind in the object of contemplation.

The first two steps, Yama and Niyama, purify and strengthen our minds through moral and ethical exercises. The third step, Âsana, is assuming postures that allow us to sit comfortably and meditate for at least an hour or two. The fourth step, Prânâyâma, is a breathing technique to control our mental and physical energies. The fifth step, Pratyâhâra, is withdrawing our minds from all objects other than the objects of meditation. The sixth step, Dhâranâ, is holding our minds with great concentration on the objects of meditation. The seventh step, Dhyâna, is a more mature form of Dhârana. And the eighth step, Samâdhi, is concentration par excellence. During Samâdhi we experience God. Samâdhi is of various kinds and will be described later. The highest type of Samâdhi is Asamprajnâta Samâdhi, also called Yoga by Patanjali.

IV

YAMA

The First Step to Yoga

Our first duty when we begin to meditate is to strengthen our mental muscles—to develop greater will power. This can be done by practicing various moral and ethical disciplines. As students of meditation, we need strong will power to protect ourselves from the lure of sense objects. If trapped by these lures, it will not be possible for us to meditate properly and have God-vision—the highest goal of meditation. The first step, Yama, consists of restraining harmful physical urges, and unwholesome thoughts and impulses. This restraint eventually helps develop tremendous will power. Yama consists of the following five practices:

1. Non-Killing

All forms of life are sacred. Violence committed even in utmost secrecy will never go unpunished. Killers cannot escape the inexorable Law of Karma—also called the Law of Cause and Effect. Terrible suffering will come to them either in this life or hereafter as the effect of their evil deeds. Spiritual seekers, therefore, must avoid killing or committing violence. Nor should they approve of any kind of violence committed by others.

Human beings are a combination of the brute, the human, and the divine. Our divine part is the soul. Selfish activities performed instinctively are expressions of our brutish nature. No rational thinking is involved in these activities; they are prompted only by blind animal urges. Activities inspired by our rational thinking are expressions of our human nature. And unselfish activities done out of genuine love and compassion for others are expressions of our divine nature. Killing or destroying other lives is caused by extreme selfishness, uncontrolled rage, or animal impulses. Killing reduces a person to the level of a beast. The goal of meditation is to manifest our divine potential by transcending our human and animal natures. For this reason a student of meditation must not kill.

However, it may be argued that just in order to live we have to be directly or indirectly involved in killing or destroying other life forms. We cannot survive without food. All food sources—whether animal or vegetable—have life in them. In order to eat we must destroy lives. Every time we breathe we kill many airborne microscopic life forms. Is it ever possible to avoid committing violence? To protect their country, soldiers kill their enemies on the battlefield. Is such killing bad? People sometimes shoot and kill robbers to protect their families. Is this good or bad? Surgeons perform surgery to cure patients, yet sometimes patients die as a result of the surgery. Are the surgeons murderers?

Each case must be judged on its individual merits. The criteria to judge these cases should be the mental attitudes with which the different acts of violence were committed. No work in itself is either good or bad; the attitude with which work is done determines whether it is good or bad. If soldiers kill the enemy on the battlefield to protect their countrymen, and are prepared to sacrifice their own lives for their country—this attitude is not selfish and such action is not considered bad. For the same reason, killing robbers to protect the family in an extreme situation may be condoned by society. When surgeons perform surgery to save the lives of their patients, they are not considered murderers if the patient dies. On the other hand, people with selfish motives who kill innocent people are murderers, and will be punished for their crimes.

In this context one thing has to be clearly understood. Even though it is virtually impossible to completely avoid committing violence, this injunction against killing is meant to minimize the tendency towards violence by developing a nonviolent attitude of mind. This is what we are expected to do. A mind with violent tendencies is not suitable for meditation.

2. Truthfulness

Truthfulness means truthfulness in thought, speech and action. The practice of truthfulness generates great mental strength. Selfishness is the major obstacle to the practice of truthfulness.

There are two types of truthfulness—convenient and inconvenient truthfulness. It is easy to practice truthfulness as long as it is convenient. Yet, when truthfulness is inconvenient, it is hard to be truthful. Some people returning from trips abroad lie to the customs officers to escape paying duty on the expensive goods they are bringing back. Truthfulness in that situation is not convenient for them, so they lie. Had they been less selfish they would not mind paying the duty. The practice of truthfulness means being truthful under all circumstances, even if inconvenient.

Shrî Krishna

Hindu tradition says in general, however, that only pleasant truths should be spoken, not unpleasant.[1] Yet, beneficial unpleasant truths may be spoken. Genuine well-wishers, such as parents and spiritual teachers, may tell unpleasant truths to their children or students to protect them from harm.

In this connection a question may be raised: Should we practice truthfulness that is harmful to others? When truthfulness endangers the lives of innocent people, should we be truthful? This point has been discussed by Shrî Krishna, a Divine Incarnation, in the story of Kaushika in the great Hindu epic, the *Mahâbhârata*,[2] which is considered a scripture of Hinduism.

The ascetic[3] Kaushika lived in a hut in a forest and performed intense spiritual austerities. He had taken the vow of truthfulness and earned the reputation that nothing could persuade him to swerve from truth. One day some terrified people came running up to him and said, "Sir, we're being chased by robbers. They want to kill us. Please let us hide here!" So saying, they hid themselves in the dense forest near the ascetic's hut. Shortly thereafter the robbers arrived and asked Kaushika if he had seen the people they were chasing. Kaushika, who was avowed to truthfulness, said, "Yes, I've seen them. They're hiding in that forest." The robbers then searched the forest, found those innocent people, and killed them. In course of time

---

1. "Satyam bruyât, priyam bruyât, mâ bruyât satyam apriyam" or "The truth should be spoken; what is pleasant should be spoken; the truth which is unpleasant should not be spoken."
2. This story is in the Karna Parva of the *Mahâbhârata*.
3. An ascetic is not necessarily a perfected Yogî who has experienced God.

when Kaushika died, he had to go to hell for causing the death of those people by his truthfulness.

Referring to this story Shrî Krishna said, "An extreme situation like this may not allow a person to remain quiet but force him to speak. Remaining quiet may be life-threatening for him. On the other hand, if he tells the truth, his truthfulness may cause the death of innocent people. Under the circumstances, it is better for him to lie. Such lying is as good as speaking the truth. Those who understand the deeper meaning of righteousness do not see any unrighteousness in one who lies in order to save innocent lives."

Shrî Krishna also said, "Our scriptures enjoin that everyone must speak the truth. In our religion no spiritual austerity is considered superior to the practice of truthfulness. Yet, it is sometimes difficult to determine how to practice truthfulness in extreme situations. In a situation where telling a lie is as spiritually beneficial as speaking the truth, and being truthful is as spiritually harmful as telling an untruth, there is no harm in lying."

It should be clearly understood that Shrî Krishna's instruction here is only for average righteous people. Unless the situation is extreme we must never lie. However, perfected Yogîs who have experienced God must never deviate from truth. Having acquired the firm conviction that they are not the body-mind complex, but the birthless and deathless Eternal Soul, they are not afraid of death. If confronted with extreme situations similar to that of Kaushika, they would try to save the lives of the innocent people by telling the robbers that they will not give them any information even if the robbers threaten to kill them.

Kaushika was an ascetic; he was not a spiritually illumined soul. Perhaps the best solution for him would have been to tell the robbers that he had never seen those people. This lie would have saved his own life and also the lives of those innocent people. Then he could have said to God, "O God, I've told a lie to save the lives of innocent people. Please give me whatever punishment I deserve for this transgression. I shall gladly accept the punishment."

In Sanskrit, the practice of truthfulness is called Satya-rakshâ—the protection of truth. Those who are established in truthfulness practice Satya-vâditâ—speaking the truth. Yogîs established in truthfulness are truthful in thought, word, and deed. They never deviate from truth even in their dreams. Truthfulness becomes second nature to them. Not only that, whatever they say comes true. Such a Yogî is called a Satya-vâdî.

3. Non-Stealing

The criterion to judge spirituality is unselfishness. Stealing is an extremely selfish act. Taking something that rightfully belongs to someone else degrades a person spiritually and, therefore, it should be avoided. Moreover, Patanjali says, "To a Yogî who is established in the practice of non-stealing, all the precious gems (i.e. wealth) of the world will come."[4] This statement has a deeper meaning. Stealing is prompted by a sense of want. Driven by this sense of want, a person covets another person's property

---

4. "Asteyapratishthâyâm sarvaratnopasthâpanam."—*Yoga-Sûtras,* 2/37.

or wealth. Poverty is no other than a sense of want. Anyone coveting wealth is actually poor. A person with no craving for wealth is truly its master and is the wealthiest of people.

4. Celibacy

Students of meditation wanting to experience God have to practice celibacy. Celibacy is conservation of energy. People have only a limited amount of physical and mental energy at their disposal. If this energy is wasted through unrestrained sexual activity, talking too much unnecessarily, and other kinds of similar physical and mental abuse, it will not be possible for them to save enough energy for the practice of meditation. It takes a great deal of energy to gain complete control over the mind. Without such control it is not possible to have the most mature form of meditation called Samâdhi. Students of meditation experience God through Samâdhi.

Celibacy for monastics

For a monk or a nun, celibacy means completely abstaining from sexual activity. Not all are cut out to be monks or nuns. Only a very small number of people are fit for monastic life. The Hindu scriptures speak of some people born with a natural yearning for spiritual life. They are devoid of any strong sex urge. The scriptures say that their sex urge was satiated in their previous incarnations. As a result, that craving is gone. They alone are fit to be monks or nuns. A true monk does not hate women; nor does a true nun hate men. If a man hates women, he secretly craves them. The same is true of a woman who hates men. True monks or nuns respect members of the other sex and look upon them as veritable manifestations of Divinity.

For them abstinence is as natural as breathing. They need no moral compulsion to practice celibacy. Those unable to practice total abstinence are not fit to be monastics. They should become householders.

Celibacy for married people

For a married couple celibacy does not mean total abstinence. It only means restrained sexual activity. This is the instruction of the Hindu scriptures. Understanding that sexual excesses drain a considerable amount of energy, an optimum amount of restraint with mutual consent between the husband and wife has to be exercised in order not to jeopardize their marriage. In course of time it will be possible for them to be one hundred percent celibate.

Other benefits of celibacy

Other than the conservation of precious physical and mental energy, celibacy has many wonderful benefits. According to the Hindu sages, celibacy enhances vigor,[5] increases the capacity of the brain, sharpens memory, and enables the celibate person to understand the deeper and subtler meaning of the scriptures. This ability to comprehend the deeper meaning of the scriptures is called Dhâranâ Shakti in Sanskrit. To grow spiritually we must acquire this ability. Acquisition of Dhâranâ Shakti enhances spiritual progress and hastens God-realization.

There are some who interpret scriptural texts literally, without understanding their deeper underlying import. They turn into religious fanatics and do immense harm to the world by their fanaticism. Had they practiced celibacy they would have the ability to understand the deeper

---

5. "Brahmacharya pratishthâyâm vîryalâbhah" which means "Through abstinence vigor is gained."—*Yoga-Sûtras*, 2/38.

meaning of the scriptural texts and would behave differently. No religion teaches hatred. Every religion teaches its followers to have love, compassion and sympathy for their fellow human beings. Deeper understanding of the scriptures would remove the possibility of harm caused by fanaticism.

Yogîs speak of a very special energy named Ojas. Of all the energies contained in the human body this is the highest. Swâmî Vivekânanda in his book *Râja Yoga* writes:[6]

> This Ojas is stored up in the brain, and the more Ojas a man has, the more powerful he is, the more intellectual, the more spiritually strong. One man may express beautiful thoughts in beautiful language, but cannot impress people. Another man may not be able to give beautiful expression to his thoughts, yet his words charm; every movement of his is powerful. That is the power of Ojas.

> Now in every man there is stored up more or less of this Ojas. The highest form of all the forces that are working in the body is Ojas.... The Yogîs say that that part of human energy which is expressed through sexual action and sexual thought, when checked and controlled, easily becomes changed into Ojas.... It is only the chaste man or woman who can create Ojas and store it in the brain; that is why chastity has always been considered the highest virtue.... That is why, in all the religious orders in the world which have produced spiritual giants, you will always find absolute chastity insisted upon.

---

6. Swâmî Vivekânanda, *Râja Yoga* (Râmakrishna-Vivekânanda Center, New York, 1982), 63-64.

Society and the practice of celibacy

The moral and ethical aspects of celibacy relate to society. The celibacy of householders implies that marital fidelity should be observed. They must not be promiscuous. Promiscuity and lack of fidelity disintegrate families and do immense harm to society. The celibacy of monastics—the practice of total abstinence—implies that they must not have sexual activity of any kind. Celibacy also means not hurting anyone by improper sexual behavior whether through speech or action.

Lustfulness and its varieties

Lustfulness is called Manasija in Sanskrit. The word literally means something that is born in the mind. Improper sexual behavior is caused by unbridled lustfulness. As lustfulness first originates in the mind as a thought, such thoughts should be nipped in the bud. Constantly chanting the holy name of God is a proven method of preventing unwholesome thoughts from arising in the mind. The *Daksha Samhitâ,* a scripture of Hinduism, says that lustfulness is expressed in eight different ways:

(i)   Thinking lustfully of someone
(ii) Talking lustfully about someone
(iii) Playing lustfully with members of the opposite sex
(iv) Looking at someone lustfully
(v)   Talking lustfully with someone in secrecy
(vi) Indulging in sexual fantasies
(vii) Making sexual advances
(viii) Getting pleasure from the sexual act

A truly celibate person must avoid all of them.

Why lustfulness is harmful for spiritual life

Those who do not believe in celibacy often criticize the scriptures for prescribing celibacy. They say that the human race will be wiped out if everyone becomes abstinent. This hypothetical and extremely remote possibility goes against the realistic world-view of the scriptures. No scripture, whether Hindu or otherwise, advocates abstinence for all people. That would be unrealistic. Abstinence is prescribed only for an extremely small number of people who are fit to be monastics. It is not meant for others. Nor is celibacy meant for people without genuine spiritual craving. The scriptures only advise sincere spiritual seekers to be celibate. If we honestly and impartially analyze lustfulness, we shall discover that it is rooted in selfishness. A lustful person craves his or her own pleasure by using someone else. When the usefulness of one person is over, the lustful person often seeks the company of another. This is promiscuity, and the scriptures of all the major religions have condemned it. Promiscuity is socially disruptive and ethically and morally harmful to mankind, because it is blatantly selfish.

Marriage is considered a sacrament by religion. Householders are expected to be faithful to their spouses. Both husband and wife are expected to make willing and loving self-sacrifice for each other. Rather than seeking their own pleasure, each spouse should try to give joy and pleasure to the other. This kind of loving sacrifice alone will make the marriage a success and turn it into a sacred relationship. Nothing else will.

A good husband is he who makes willing and loving self-sacrifice for his wife. The same is true for a good wife. I have not met a single person who loves selfish people.

How can a wife or husband be selfish and yet expect to be loved by her or his spouse? And if there be no love between them, how can their marriage last? All sociologists will agree that broken marriages are a disease of society. Young children go through terrible psychological trauma when they see their parents separate or divorce. Feeling unduly deprived of the parental love that they took for granted, some may turn out to be unloving and cruel. Others may become excessively demanding of love and affection from others, or lose faith in all human love. Still others may fall into bad company and become drug addicts, alcoholics, or criminals. At the very least, deep down in their hearts they may suffer from a persistent sadness caused by the separation of their parents. Many of the emotional problems adults suffer from can be traced to childhoods spent in broken homes. They often repeat the pattern set by their parents and enter into marriages that easily break up, making their children casualties in the same vicious circle.

The family is the indispensable, basic unit of society. The foundation of all social institutions throughout the whole world is this family unit. And the most important members of this unit are the children, who are the future of humanity. Unless they have proper upbringing they will not grow up to be caring and responsible adults. They will not be able to carry out their social responsibilities properly. As a result, society will become degraded. Who is responsible for this? How to avoid this painful social tragedy? Unless parents have higher ideals their selfishness will continue to devastate society, and the world will be a terrible place to live in. Prophets and scriptures of all religions try to prevent that dreadful possibility by asking people to become a little less selfish and a little more loving and caring.

5. Nonacceptance of unnecessary gifts

Accepting unnecessary gifts causes loss of freedom. Those who receive gifts become obliged to the giver. Unscrupulous people sometimes give gifts, secretly intending to obligate the recipients. The recipients may feel obliged to return the favor by doing even unethical things. Obligation is a form of slavery. It robs people of their freedom and generates mental degradation. A serious student of meditation must avoid accepting unnecessary gifts as much as practicable.

V

NIYAMA

The Second Step To Yoga

Niyama is the cultivation of the following good habits to improve the quality of the mind and make it stronger, among these are:

1. *Keeping the body and mind clean*

A spiritual seeker should maintain external and internal cleanliness. The body as well as the mind should be kept clean and pure. A dirty person can never be a Yogî. Then again, a person is more mind than body. Of the two, more emphasis should be put on developing a pure mind.

Pure mind—and how to acquire it

What is this pure mind? To answer this I have to first explain a very well-known term in Indian philosophy called Guna. This term was first used by the Sânkhya School, believed to be the oldest among the six major schools of philosophy developed in India.[1] According to this school, the entire cosmos—animate and inanimate—has evolved from the primordial subtle matter called Prakriti. All forms of matter, energy, and also the mind are

---

1. The other five schools of Hindu philosophy are Pûrva Mîmâmsâ, Uttara Mîmâmsâ (or Vedânta), Yoga, Nyâya and Vaisheshika.

the evolved products of Prakriti. Prakriti can also be loosely called Mother Nature.

The three Gunas

Prakriti or Mother Nature is composed of three extremely subtle substances, each of which is a Guna. *Guna*, a Sanskrit word, has more than one meaning. It usually means quality, but in this context it means a string or strand. If we think of Prakriti as a rope made of three strands, then each strand is a Guna. The names of these three Gunas are Sattwa, Rajas and Tamas.

The Gunas can only be known indirectly

Each Guna has its own characteristic properties. The Gunas are extremely subtle and cannot be directly perceived by our sense organs. The presence of the Gunas can only be known indirectly by noticing their properties manifested through their evolved products. It is like knowing the presence of electricity by seeing its manifestation in electrical gadgets. Electricity is invisible to the naked eye and its presence cannot be known directly.

Characteristics of the Gunas

Sattwa is of the nature of joy, and is light (i.e., not heavy), buoyant, bright or illuminating. It has the power to enlighten or reveal things. The various types of joy—satisfaction, pleasure, contentment, happiness, bliss, etc.—that we experience from different objects of pleasure show that Sattwa is present in them, as well as in our minds which enjoy them. The lightness of hot air balloons and the highly buoyant cork indicate the presence of Sattwa in them. The luminosity of light and flames show that Sattwa is present in them. The presence of Sattwa causes our minds to be alert, aware, peaceful, compassionate, serene, and capable of knowing the unknown. Whenever we come to know anything, the revelation of that knowledge is due to the presence of Sattwa in our minds.

Rajas causes movement, activity and stimulation. Wherever there is any activity or movement, Rajas is present. Rajas also generates restlessness, pain, and suffering. Anger, self-conceit, arrogance, boastfulness, the tendency to dominate over others, etc., indicate the presence of Rajas in our minds.

The properties of Tamas are the very opposite of those of Sattwa and Rajas. While Sattwa causes lightness and the ability to acquire knowledge, Tamas produces heaviness and obstructs knowledge by ignorance. While Sattwa contributes to mental peace and serenity, Tamas induces dullness and confusion. Sattwa endows light with the power to dispel darkness. Tamas causes darkness. While Rajas produces activity, restlessness, and enthusiasm, Tamas brings laziness, passivity, drowsiness, apathy, lack of enthusiasm, and mental depression.

The Gunas, though differing in their properties, share two common characteristics. The first is that the Gunas, like three young siblings, are always playfully wrestling with one another. Each struggles to make itself predominant by subduing the other two. As a result of that ongoing struggle, sometimes Sattwa becomes predominant, sometimes Rajas, and sometimes Tamas. This explains why the mental and physical states of ordinary people tend to fluctuate and are not stable. Sometimes the body feels very light, and the mind is extremely alert and serene—indicating the preponderance of Sattwa. Sometimes the body feels energetic while the mind is restless—indicating that Rajas has become predominant. At other times both the body and mind may be sluggish and lethargic—denoting the preponderance of Tamas.

The second characteristic is that despite their perpetual struggle the Gunas cooperate and help one another. No single Guna can exist independently of the other two; they are always together. Their cooperation is very much like the cooperation between the wax, wick and flame of a lighted candle. Without the cooperation of the wax and the wick no candle flame is possible.

The Gunas constitute the entire cosmos

As stated earlier, the entire cosmos is the evolved form of Prakriti or Mother Nature. And Prakriti is no other than the three Gunas. All forms of matter, energy—and even the mind—are the evolved products of the three Gunas. Gunas are subtler and finer than anything we know in this world. Yet they become this entire gross world through evolution.[2]

Sattwa Guna is essential for purity of mind

Most of the time a perfected Yogî's mind has a preponderance of Sattwa and is serene, calm, compassionate, alert and non-violent. It is not deluded or confused like a mind dominated by Tamas. Nor is it restless, conceited, and domineering like a mind dominated by Rajas. This is the pure mind which enables us to experience God. By

_____

2. To know more about how the Gunas constitute the entire cosmos see Chapter XIV.

intense spiritual practice alone can such a mind be achieved.

In this context we may ask, "One falls asleep only when Tamas is predominant in one's body and mind. Since a Yogî's mind has a preponderance of Sattwa most of the time, is it possible for a Yogî to have adequate sleep?" The answer is that a Yogî does sleep, but the sleep is very light. Having a mind tending naturally toward meditation, a perfected Yogî's mind and body enjoy great rest and peace during meditation. Therefore, very little sleep is needed.

Samskâras or impressions of past thoughts

There is another important factor connected with the process of mental purification. No thought is ever lost. All our past thoughts remain stored in the unconscious domain of our minds. They remain there as Samskâras or impressions. If the mind be compared to a lake, all the impressions of our past thoughts—good or bad—are lying at its bottom. For mental purification all these Samskâras must be eliminated, in addition to making Sattwa Guna preponderant.

How to eliminate Samskâras

The mind is like a self-cleaning oven. It can clean itself by getting rid of its Samskâras. Only a concentrated mind can eliminate Samskâras. When a concentrated mind chants the holy name of God (Japa), or engages in meditation (Dhyâna), it penetrates into its unconscious domain and dislodges the Samskâras. The Samskâras then rise to the conscious level of the mind and disappear forever. The following analogy will explain how that happens.

Let us imagine a person standing on the shore of a lake. The water is muddy. It also has many waves in it. At the bottom of the lake there is a bright light. The person standing on the shore cannot see the light because the muddy water obstructs it. In this analogy the lake is the mind; the waves symbolize restlessness created by Rajas; and the turbidity of water is ignorance and mental confusion caused by Tamas. The bright light at the bottom of the lake is the indwelling Divine Self or the soul.

The person on the shore is holding a bundle of absorbent paper towels and is throwing them one by one into the lake. The towels first float on the surface, absorb moisture, and then sink to the bottom. They settle at the bottom forming layer after layer; not a single one is lost. Each paper towel is a thought. When floating, it is a conscious thought; when submerged, it is a Samskâra or a subconscious thought.

Then again each Samskâra is like a seed. Given the right circumstances a seed has the power to become a tree. Similarly, every Samskâra has the power to become a conscious thought again if it can be brought up to the conscious level. A highly concentrated mind is like a laser beam. It can go deep down into the subconscious. When such a mind meditates or chants the holy name of God, it acts like a deep-water probe and starts disturbing and dislodging some of the accumulated Samskâras. As a result, they float up to the surface and turn into conscious thoughts. The meditator is advised not to act upon these rejuvenated thoughts, but to only watch them like a disinterested observer. Then the thoughts will disappear and never return again. This is how most of the Samskâras can be eliminated and the mind made pure. The finer residual Samskâras, however, are extremely subtle and can only be destroyed by the deepest concentration called Asamprajnâta Samâdhi.

We may ask, "Is it possible to know which thoughts arising in our minds during meditation are rejuvenated Samskâras, and which are new thoughts?" To answer this I have to point out that revitalized past thoughts are recollected thoughts. They have been retrieved from the subconscious domain. New thoughts are not recollections. Yet, it is not always possible to ascertain which are revitalized Samskâras and which are new thoughts. Some revitalized Samskâras may be very ancient. The soul carries along with it the same mind from incarnation to incarnation, and some thoughts that arise in the mind during meditation may be revitalized Samskâras from past incarnations.[3] Therefore, our main task during meditation should be to hold on to the object of our meditation, for both revitalized past thoughts (Samskâras) and new intruding thoughts are distractions.

The light of the soul, the Divine Self, reveals itself without any distortions when the waves of the mind subside, the turbidity in the water is gone, and all the submerged paper towels or Samskâras are eliminated. Calming the waves down is overcoming Rajas; removing the turbidity of the water is making Sattwa dominant by overcoming Tamas; and eliminating the sunken paper towels is cleansing the mind of its Samskâras. A pure mind is a mind with

---

3. According to Hinduism, when a person dies his or her soul departs from the physical body along with the mind, the senses and the vital energy. It is the same mind that incarnates again.

a preponderance of Sattwa, rid of all but the finer, extremely subtle, residual Samskâras. As stated earlier, those Samskâras can be got rid of only in Asamprajnâta Samâdhi.[4]

Another frequently used analogy is that of an inkwell. Its ink has dried up due to evaporation. The dried-up ink is clinging to the inner wall of the inkwell. In this analogy the inkwell is the unconscious domain of the mind, while the dried ink represents the Samskâras. One method of cleaning the inkwell is to put it under a faucet and allow water to run into it. The running water will gradually flush the ink out and make the inkwell spotlessly clean. The running water represents the concentrated mind of the meditator. It can help eliminate Samskâras and make the mind pure.

A pure mind enables us to experience God

Mental purity is essential for God-realization. The Hindu scriptures say that an impure mind cannot know God. The pure mind alone can help us experience God. Christianity echoes this thought as well. Jesus said, "Blessed are the pure in heart, for they shall see God."[5] Pure heart is no other than the pure mind. No physical eyes are needed to see God. Even a blind person can see or experience God with the inner eyes or the pure mind. God in His truest state is formless. He is beyond time, space and causation. Having transcended time, God is eternal. Having transcended space, God is infinite. Being free from the ceaseless change generated by causation, God is changeless.

---

4. To know about Asamprajnâta Samâdhi see Chapter XV.
5. The Gospel according to St. Matthew, 5:8.

How a pure mind helps us experience God can be explained by an analogy. Ice, water and water vapor are one and the same substance. Yet in their properties they are very different from one another. Ice has the least amount of freedom. A chunk of ice cannot move, it will stay wherever it has been put. On the other hand, water enjoys more freedom than ice. It can flow and spread out. Water vapor, being a gas, has the greatest amount of freedom. It can easily fill up a large room. Besides that, it is invisible and is the subtlest of the three.

Like ice, the average mind has many limitations. Due to these limitations it cannot know God. A pure mind, like water vapor, is beyond such limitations. It can help us to know God through direct experience. Direct experience generates unshakeable conviction. It is like our conviction that we exist. No amount of persuasion by others can dislodge this conviction. So also is the knowledge of God acquired by the pure mind. When we directly experience God, all our doubts are dispelled forever.

Maintaining physical cleanliness

Now let us discuss why in addtion to acquiring a pure mind the body also has to be kept clean. According to Patanjali, physical cleanliness helps in reducing lustfulness. This is the primary reason why physical cleanliness has to be observed. When the attempt is made to keep the body meticulously clean, it becomes increasingly obvious that it does not stay clean for long. The various biological functions such as perspiration, evacuation, etc., continually soil it. No matter how many times the body is washed and cleaned, it becomes dirty again. Having observed the body's natural tendency to become unclean, distaste for the body is gradually developed. This realization brings the awareness of the unclean state of other people's bodies as well. Thus, by the practice of external purification, distaste is developed for having intimate physical relationships with others. This is the view of Patanjali who also says that from the practice of cleanliness the preponderance of Sattwa Guna arises, bringing on cheerfulness, concentration, conquest of the sense organs, and fitness for the realization of the Divine Self.[6] In his book *Râja Yoga* Swâmî Vivekânanda explains these views of Patanjali:

> When there is real purification of the body, there arises neglect of the body; the idea of keeping it nice vanishes. A face which others call most beautiful will appear to the Yogî as merely an animal face if the Spirit is not behind it. What the world calls a very common face he will regard as heavenly if the Spirit shines behind it. The thirst after the body is the great bane of human life. So the first sign of the attainment of purity is that you do not care to think you are a body. It is only when purity comes that we get rid of the idea of the body.

In other words, a person cannot be body-conscious and God-conscious at the same time. However, this distaste or neglect in regard to the body does not make a person lose interest in maintaining physical cleanliness, nor become unloving and apathetic towards others. A Yogî never lacks love and affection for other human beings, whether they are physically clean or unclean. The Yogî is always eager to serve them, realizing that even inside their unclean bodies shines that ever-pure Divine Spirit. Serving them is as

---

6. *Yoga-Sûtras*, 2/40-41.

good as serving God. The unselfish love of a perfected Yogî is expressed through kindness, compassion, sympathy, friendliness and an intense desire for the well-being of others. This love is not camouflaged lust. Lustfulness is inherently selfish. A lustful person seeks sensual gratification by using others. A Yogî loves others without expecting anything in return.

However, there is one problem with maintaining external cleanliness. Sometimes people go to extremes and become obsessed with the idea of bodily cleanliness. Like obsessive-compulsive people they develop a mania about it. A preponderance of Sattwa-Guna enables a person to think clearly and rationally. In mental obsession there is no rational thinking. An obsession with physical cleanliness does not indicate a preponderance of Sattwa-Guna. Rational thinking and following the path of moderation can prevent or cure this obsession.

2. Being content with the bare necessities of life

One who is content with the bare necessities of life gets peace of mind. Patanjali says, "...from contentment comes superlative happiness."[7] Greed is a major obstacle to contentment. It is born out of selfishness and can never be satiated. Driven by greed, people run after more and more enjoyment. Besides bringing frequent disappointment, such pursuits are an unnecessary waste of energy and make the mind restless. A restless mind is unfit for meditation.

---

7. *Yoga-Sûtras*, 2/42.

3. Getting used to physical and mental austerities

Generally speaking, there are two types of austerity—physical and mental. Austerity can be defined as restraints willingly imposed upon the body or mind. The practice of austerity strengthens both the body and mind. The average person's body and mind are closely entwined. If anything happens to the body, the mind is affected. Similarly, the body becomes affected when something happens to the mind. However, the practice of austerity and other spiritual disciplines strengthens the mind and brings it under control. The body no longer can affect a controlled mind. It now becomes possible for a person to meditate deeply without any interference from the body.

The *Bhagavad Gîtâ* speaks of three types of austerity:

- Austerity of the body
- Austerity of speech
- Austerity of the mind

Worshiping God; adoring holy people, spiritual teachers, and the wise through salutations, etc.; maintaining physical purity; straightforward behavior; practicing celibacy; and refraining from committing violence are austerities of the body.[8] Occasional fasting, not indulging in sensual pleasures, subjecting the body to occasional strain and hardship for spiritual reasons, learning to remain unaffected by heat or cold, are also considered physical austerities. One not easily affected by physical discomforts is mentally a stronger person. Thus physical austerity also contributes to developing mental strength.

---

8. "Deva-dvija-guru-prâjna-pûjanam shaucham ârjavam/brahmacharyam ahimsâ cha shârîram tapa ûchyate."—*Bhagavad Gîtâ*, 17/14.

Speaking words that are true, inoffensive, pleasant, and beneficial, as well as regular chanting of the scriptures, are called austerities of speech.[9]

Trying to make the mind calm and serene, being gentle, controlling one's thoughts in order to minimize unnecessary talking, self-control and honesty of purpose are austerities of the mind.[10]

4. Regular study of the scriptures and chanting the holy name of God (Swâdhyâya)

Regular study of the scriptures helps prevent the mind from sliding down and being influenced by negative forces and the distracting lure of the senses. According to Patanjali, repeatedly chanting the holy name of God enables the spiritual aspirant to eventually experience God.[11]

5. The practice of surrendering to God (Îshwara-pranidhâna)

Much spiritual practice is needed to develop the ability to truly surrender to God. After following spiritual disciplines for a long time a spiritual aspirant may make great progress and yet not have God-vision. At this stage the realization comes that by one's own strength alone it is not possible to reach the spiritual goal. The aspirant feels extremely helpless and sincerely yearns for God's help.

---

9. "Anudvega-karam vâkyam satyam priya-hitam cha yat/ svâdhyâyâbhyasanam chaiva vângmayam tapa uchyate."— *Bhagavad Gîtâ*, 17/15.

10. "Manah-prasâdah saumyatvam maunam âtma-vinigrahah/ bhâva-samsuddhir ity-etat tapo Mânasam uchyate."—*Bhagavad Gîtâ*, 17/16.

11. *Yoga-Sûtras*, 2/44.

Then alone does a true spirit of self-surrender develop, and it becomes possible to take refuge in God. The following analogy will make this idea clear:

The pilot of a small aircraft was flying over the Sahara desert. Suddenly the engine died and the plane nose-dived. A crash was inevitable. Luckily, the pilot had a parachute; he bailed out of the plane and landed safely on the desert.

He had with him a small bottle of water, a compass, and a map. Studying the map he located an oasis sixty miles away. Walking for three days in the relative coolness of night and resting in the daytime he came within a mile of the oasis. He clearly saw a small lake with some date trees and huts around it. He was dead tired. He had been without food for three days and was extremely thirsty. Somehow he dragged himself along over the hot sand and finally arrived a short distance away from the lake. There he lay on the sand, completely exhausted. The lake was only a few feet away, yet he could not reach it. Utterly helpless and almost dying of thirst, he realized that none other than God could help him in that situation. He then completely surrendered to God and with all his heart and soul prayed to Him for help.

Only in a similar situation can one truly surrender to God, not otherwise. According to Patanjali one can even attain the deepest Samâdhi—the acme of spiritual illumination—by true resignation or surrender to God.[12,13]

---

12. See Chapter XV to know more about Samâdhi.
13. *Yoga-Sûtras*, 2/45.

VI

ÂSANA
The Third Step to Yoga

The third step, Âsana, means a suitable posture in which a person can sit comfortably for a long time and meditate. Sitting with the backbone erect, the chest, neck and head should be held vertically in a straight line. The teacher may instruct the student to sit in this posture and meditate for a set duration each day, preferably at the same time. The people of India, Myanmar, Srî Lanka and other Asian countries learn to sit cross-legged from their early childhood. This makes it easier for them to sit that way for meditation. They also seem to have more flexible joints. Bodies and constitutions differ, and the same meditation posture may not be suitable for everybody. For most Western people, sitting comfortably in a straight-backed arm-chair with good lumbar support may be more suitable. There is no hard and fast rule about how one should sit for meditation. No matter which posture is chosen, the backbone must be kept erect, and the chest, neck and head held vertically in a straight line.

The Yoga scriptures speak of various kinds of Âsana: Padmâsana, Vajrâsana, Gomukhâsana, Siddhâsana, Vîrâsana, etc. If interested, one can learn these postures from qualified teachers.

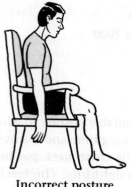
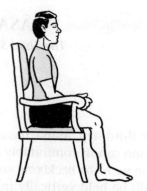

**Incorrect posture
for meditation**

**Correct posture
for meditation**

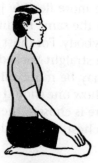

Vajrâsana

Padmâsana
(Lotus Posture)

One who can sit firmly and comfortably in a Yoga posture continuously for at least three hours is called an Âsana-Siddha. The expression Âsana-Siddha means a person who has gained mastery over an Âsana or Yoga posture. The true sign of an Âsana-Siddha is that there will be no awareness of the body even after sitting for hours in a Yoga posture. On the other hand, someone without such mastery will experience various physical discomforts. Either the legs or feet will go to sleep; or the back, shoulders, or neck will start hurting. These physical discomforts will surely bring an acute awareness of the body and interfere with meditation. This is why we need a comfortable Âsana or sitting posture for meditation.

VII

PRÂNÂYÂMA
The Fourth Step to Yoga

What is Prânâyâma?

Prânâyâma is a rhythmic breathing exercise. If done properly, it may help a restless or dissipated mind become calm and concentrated. The exercise consists in breathing in slowly through the left nostril, say, for five seconds; then holding the breath for twenty seconds; and finally releasing it slowly for ten seconds through the right nostril. The second time the process has to be reversed. This time air has to be inhaled for five seconds through the right nostril, the breath should then be held for twenty seconds, and finally the breath should be released for ten seconds through the left nostril. Inhaling is called in Sanskrit Pûraka; holding the breath is Kumbhaka; and exhaling is Rechaka. The whole process is called Prânâyâma. The person practicing Prânâyâma has to repeat this process a few times.

Dangers associated with the practice of Prânâyâma

Prânâyâma should be practiced under the strict guidance of a genuine teacher, otherwise it can be extremely dangerous. I saw a schoolteacher in India turn completely insane by practicing Prânâyâma without a guide. I knew a medical doctor who practiced Prânâyâma for several years without the guidance of a proper teacher. As a result, he developed total amnesia. Another gentleman developed premature old age practicing Prânâyâma on his own. Illnesses caused by the improper practice of Prânâyâma cannot easily be cured by conventional medicines.

Lately in the West questionable teachers indifferent to these dangers have started teaching Prânâyâma. Once a young woman came to see me in Seattle. She introduced herself as a Yoga teacher and mentioned that she taught Prânâyâma.

"Where did you learn Yoga?" I enquired.

She replied, "I've learned it through a correspondence course offered by a Yoga group in India." Then she showed me a certificate given by that group stating that she was competent to teach Yoga.

"How much money did they charge for the course?" I asked her.

"A considerable amount," answered the girl.

On further enquiry I was appalled to hear that the Yoga group had never cautioned her that Prânâyâma, if practiced improperly, could be extremely hazardous. It is unfortunate that organizations are mushrooming in India, as well as in the West, with the sole purpose of exploiting people either for money or to gain control over them. They entrap people by exploiting their psychological weaknesses.

There is a saying in India: "You can get Gurus by the hundreds and thousands, but it is hard to find a single sincere disciple." This ruthless world of break-neck competition often makes a person feel insignificant and inferior. A sense of inferiority creates the desire to somehow become superior and important. And this makes the idea of becoming a teacher more appealing than becoming a student. Ill-motivated organizations exploit this weakness. For substantial fees they offer to make anyone a teacher within a short time, sometimes through mail-order courses. Mail-order instructions can surely help students seeking a secular education. But in regard to techniques for spiritual practice, particularly those that can cause harm if not practiced under the watchful eyes of a teacher, mail-order instructions are not only inadequate but dangerous as well. For their own good, students should avoid these courses.

Necessary qualifications for a student of Prânâyâma

Those seeking to practice Prânâyâma must fulfill certain requirements. They must practice celibacy; have regular bowel movements; practice moderation in food, sleep and speech; and not lead a stressful life. Most importantly, "there must be perfect chastity, in thought, word and deed," says Swâmî Vivekânanda. Unless these requirements are fulfilled, the practice of Prânâyâma can be extremely dangerous.

One person told me, "Swâmî, I practiced Prânâyâma for five minutes every day for quite some time without any harmful consequence. Why then do you say that the practice of Prânâyâma is dangerous?"

I replied, "If you take a minute dose of poison every day it may not do you any noticeable harm for awhile, but eventually you'll notice its bad effects. That's why you have to be cautious. Practicing Prânâyâma for five minutes a day may show no good or bad effects for awhile, but in course of time its effects will surely be noticeable.

For instance, one person I knew developed symptoms of premature old age from practicing Prânâyâma for only ten minutes a day. For several years he didn't notice any adverse effect. Eventually he developed a persistent headache accompanied by a gradual loss of memory. After a thorough medical investigation his doctors diagnosed the symptoms to be mainly the signs of premature old age. All this was the effect of his practice of Prânâyâma without the guidance of a proper teacher.

True meaning of the word Prânâyâma

As mentioned earlier, Prânâyâma ordinarily means a breathing exercise, but it also has a deeper meaning. The Sanskrit word *Prâna* means cosmic energy. *Ayama* means control. The compound word *Prânâyâma* means the control of this energy. A portion of this cosmic energy is present in every person and is used for all internal and external activities. These activities are thinking, breathing, eating, drinking, digesting, voiding, circulating blood throughout the body, talking or singing, moving, and creating progeny.

Although Prâna is the general name of this energy, it is given five different specialized names—Prâna, Vyâna, Apâna, Udâna and Samâna—depending upon its activities. It is called Prâna when it is used for breathing and functioning of the heart. When it causes the circulation of blood and other vital fluids throughout the body, it is called Vyâna. Similarly, Apâna is responsible for eating, drinking, voiding and procreation. Udâna is responsible for talking or singing. Samâna is responsible for digesting food. It should be clearly understood that it is the same cosmic energy, Prâna, which has been given five different names—Prâna, Vyâna, Apâna, Udâna and Samâna—depending upon it's activities in the human body.

Among all these activities breathing is the most vital. Says Swâmî Vivekânanda, a master of Yoga:

> The most obvious manifestation of this Prâna (energy) in the human body is the motion of the lungs. If that stops, as a rule all other manifestations of force (Prâna) in the body will immediately stop.

> Prânâyâma really means controlling this motion of the lungs, and this motion is associated with the breath. Not that the breath produces it; on the contrary, it (i.e. the motion of the lungs) produces the breath. This motion draws in the air by pump action. Prâna (energy) moves the lungs; the movement of the lungs draws in the air. So Prânâyâma is not breathing, but controlling that muscular power (or energy) which moves the lungs.... When the Prâna (energy) has become controlled, then we shall immediately find that all the other actions of Prâna in the body will slowly come under control.

Through Prânâyâma masters of Yoga not only control the energy in their bodies but also cosmic energy. How they control cosmic energy is explained by the following analogy: Consider a faucet in a home. Its water is coming from a large reservoir many miles away. In this analogy the faucet represents the lungs, and the reservoir the cosmic energy. If we turn the faucet on and let the water run continuously for a long time, it will have some effect on the reservoir. The water in the reservoir will get depleted, no matter how imperceptibly. By controlling the water pouring out of the faucet, one can thus indirectly control the water of the reservoir. Similarly, by controlling Prâna in the lungs through Prânâyâma, a Yogî can eventually control even cosmic Prâna (cosmic energy). But to accomplish that the Yogî will have to first totally master concentration.

A safer alternative to the practice of Prânâyâma

As there are hazards associated with the practice of Prânâyâma, a safer alternative is given by the sages of India, including Patanjali. They say that cultivating devotion to God enables a spiritual aspirant to have God-experience without practicing Prânâyâma or other Yoga techniques.[1] Through devotion, when the mind becomes concentrated on God or the chosen Deity, Kumbhaka happens automatically. Then there is no need for the practice of Prânâyâma. Thus the fourth step to Yoga can be safely skipped.

---

1. "Îshwarapranidhânâdvâ"—"Success in Yoga can be achieved by devotion to God." *Yoga-Sûtras*, 1/23.

VIII

PRATYÂHÂRA
The Fifth Step to Yoga

All the senses become attached to the objects on which they feed. The organ of sight feeds on beautiful sights and forms; the organ of hearing feeds on various sounds; the organ of smell is nourished by different smells; the organ of taste feeds on various types of food and drink; and the organ of touch thrives on tactile sensations. Pratyâhâra consists in withdrawing the senses from the objects on which they depend. Such withdrawal is possible when the mind, by exercising tremendous will-power, can control the senses. Bringing the senses under control takes a lot of practice. In the Hindu scriptures an uncontrolled mind has been compared to a drunken monkey stung by scorpions. A monkey by nature is extremely restless. When drunk and stung by scorpions, it becomes all the more agitated. How can such a mind be controlled? The following words of Swâmî Vivekânanda teach us how it can be done:

> The first lesson is to sit for some time and let the mind run on. The mind is bubbling up all the time. It is like that monkey jumping about. Let the monkey jump as much as he can; you simply wait and watch. Knowledge is power says the proverb, and that is true. Until you know what the

mind is doing you cannot control it. Give it the
rein; many hideous thoughts may come into it;
you will be astonished that it was possible for you
to think such thoughts. But you will find that
each day the mind's vagaries are becoming less
and less violent, that each day it is becoming
calmer. In the first few months you will find that
the mind will have a great many (such) thoughts,
later you will find that they have somewhat
decreased, and in a few more months they will be
fewer and fewer, until at last the mind will be
under perfect control. But we must patiently practice every day.... This controlling the mind...is
Pratyâhâra.... It is tremendous work, not to be
done in a day. Only after a patient, continuous
struggle for years can we succeed.[1]

The *Bhagavad Gîtâ* also teaches us how a restless and tur-
bulent mind can be controlled. It says that such a mind
can be controlled by relentless practice (Abhyâsa), and the
absence of desire for objects of sense pleasure (Vairâgya).[2]
When the mind has effectively controlled the senses, they
no longer run after their objects. As a result, the mind
becomes free from the distractions caused by sense
objects. It is now ready for the next higher step—Dhâranâ.

---

1. Swâmî Vivekânanda, *Râja Yoga* (Râmakrishna-Vivekânanda
Center of New York, 1982), 69-70.
2. *Bhagavad Gîtâ*, 6/35.

IX

DHÂRANÂ

The Sixth Step to Yoga

Dhâranâ is fixing the mind on the object of contemplation. That object should be something holy, such as God, a deity, or a Divine Incarnation. Dhâranâ is a preliminary stage of meditation. When we can make our mind steadfastly cling to the object of contemplation, we are ready to go to the next higher step, meditation (Dhyâna).

The practice of Dhâranâ can start with learning how to hold our mind to a certain point or part of our body to the exclusion of all other parts. For instance, we may try to think only of the thumb of our right hand to the exclusion of the rest of our body. When we can successfully do it, it is called Dhâranâ. At that point we are aware only of our right thumb, and nothing else. There is a story in the *Mahâbhârata* that makes this idea very clear. King Pându had five sons—Yudhisthira, Bhîma, Arjuna, Nakula and Sahadeva. Along with other kinds of education, they were also trained in the martial arts. Their teacher, Drona, was the most famous teacher of martial arts of that time. After several years of training, the princes became very skilled in the use of all kinds of weapons.

One day Drona decided to test the princes' skill in archery. He placed a wooden bird on a high branch of a tall tree. Then he asked his students to take their bows and arrows, aim at the bird, and cut off its head with a single arrow. Following his instructions the students placed arrows in their bows and aimed at the wooden bird.

Drona said to them, "Before you shoot tell me what you're seeing. Are you seeing the bird on the tree, as well as me and others assembled here?"

Yudhisthira, Bhîma, Nakula and Sahadeva replied, "Yes, sir, we're seeing all of you gathered here and also the bird on the tree."

Drona said, "Move aside! I'm sure none of you will hit the bird."

Only Arjuna said, "Sir, I'm seeing the bird and nothing else."

Drona said, "Concentrate more and tell me what you're seeing."

Arjuna said, "I'm now seeing only the bird's head and nothing else."

Hearing his reply Drona was well pleased. He said to Arjuna, "You'll be able to hit the target. Release your arrow!" Arjuna immediately shot his arrow and decapitated the bird. Arjuna alone among the princes had mastered the practice of Dhâranâ. He was able to fix his mind on the head of the wooden bird to the exclusion of everything else around it.

Similar examples can be borrowed from American baseball. Pitchers often throw balls that travel at a speed of nearly 100 miles per hour. To hit such a fast ball is extremely difficult. It needs extremely good eye and hand coordination. Most people playing baseball for the first time will not even be able to see the ball coming—what to speak of hitting it! But some famous professional baseball players have claimed that not only can they see the approaching fast ball clearly, but they also see the stitches on it! One player claimed that when he concentrated on the oncoming ball he saw it as much larger than its normal size. The ball appeared to him as large as a watermelon, and he had no difficulty hitting it. Yet, the diameter of a baseball is approximately 3 inches, while the diameter of a small watermelon is around 10 inches. All this can be easily explained in terms of Dhâranâ.

Dhâranâ matures into Dhyâna, and Dhyâna into Samâdhi

Fixing the mind on its object of contemplation for 12 seconds equals one measure of Dhâranâ. Twelve measures of Dhâranâ equal one measure of Dhyâna. In other words, when the mind can be kept in that state of concentration for 144 seconds (2 minutes and 24 seconds), it is called Dhyâna. Twelve measures of Dhyâna, i.e. uninterrupted concentration for 28 minutes and 48 seconds, will constitute Samâdhi. Dhâranâ, Dhyâna and Samâdhi are only different degrees of concentration. In the language of Râja Yoga, they are all Samyama (concentration).

X

DHYÂNA
Seventh Step To Yoga

Dhyâna is intense mental concentration. It is also called meditation. It is not easy to master the art of concentration. In trying to achieve it we are likely to encounter many obstacles. These have to be overcome. Most, if not all, of these obstacles are created by the mind itself. The *Bhagavad Gîtâ* says that one's mind can be one's best friend and also one's worst enemy.[1] Before beginning to practice meditation, it can be of great help to become aware of the following characteristics of the mind:

- The mind, like water, has a natural tendency to flow downward. It has an inherent inclination to do what is harmful by indulging in sensual, destructive and negative thoughts. We must constantly watch our minds and not allow them to go downward.
- The mind naturally resents being controlled or restrained.
- The mind inherently gets bored doing the same thing over and over again. It constantly craves newer and more sensational experiences.

---

1. "Âtmaiva hy-âtmano bandhur-âtmaiva ripur-âtmanah"—*Bhagavad Gîtâ*, 6/5.

- Old bad habits of the mind die hard. It takes a lot of will power and sustained effort to get rid of them.

Meditation is guided imagination of the real

In order to meditate we have to use our imagination. It cannot be random or unbridled imagination. The imagining must be done with the greatest concentration under the guidance of a genuine teacher. The other requirement is that the object of imagination has to be *real*. Sustained guided imagination of the *real* is meditation (Dhyâna). Imagining unreal objects is not meditation. It is fantasy.

What is real?

In the context of meditation it is essential to know the true meaning of the word *real*. According to Hindu philosophy, anything that is real has to fulfill two conditions. It has to be both changeless and eternal. Hindu philosophers insist that these two criteria are used even when we judge reality in our day-to-day life. Two analogies may explain this point clearly.

Let us suppose there is a creature that changes its form every three seconds. The first three seconds it is a cat, then it turns into a weasel, then into a mongoose, and then into something else. As the creature is changing its form so frequently and so fast, it is impossible for us to determine its real identity. Had the creature been changeless it would be easy to know what it really was. The changelessness of the creature would prove that it was really a cat, and not anything else.

The second analogy is of a dinosaur seen in our backyard for only five seconds. Then it vanishes into thin air.

After it disappears, we are left wondering if we were hallucinating! We cannot believe that what we saw for only five seconds was real. Had the dinosaur remained there forever, we would never have doubted its real existence. In this case we would have determined the reality of the dinosaur in terms of its perpetuity.

Hindus conceive of God as changeless and eternal. God alone is real. Everything in the world is transient and subject to change. Nothing pertaining to the world can be real. We already know that the object of meditation has to be real. As God alone is real, the object of meditation must be God.

The teacher gives proper guidance in imagining God. This type of imagining will in course of time mature and enable the student to directly experience God. The popular saying—"Today's imagination is tomorrow's realization"—is very true of meditation. How this process of guided imagination can lead to God-experience is explained by another analogy.

Let us consider a blind man who has inherited immense wealth. He wants to buy a large house for himself. A realtor comes to him to talk about a beautiful mansion that is for sale. The realtor describes the house in great detail, and hearing the description the blind man creates a vivid mental picture of the house. In this analogy the realtor is the teacher of meditation and the blind man his student. He is guiding the student in imagining the real house.

Then the realtor takes the blind man to the mansion. The buyer has already come to know the layout of the real house through his imagination and has no difficulty now in directly exploring and knowing it.

God is not only the one and only reality but is also the holiest of the holy, the purest of the pure. By meditating on the exalted holiness of God our mind gradually becomes completely holy and pure. The mental impurity that temporarily covers the effulgent sun of divinity in us like a cloud is dispelled forever. Our inherent divinity now blazes forth in its boundless glory. This is the acme of spiritual progress—reaching the ultimate goal of meditation. This is spiritual illumination.

What we meditate on, we become

Mahendranâth Datta, the younger brother of Swâmî Vivekânanda, was a scholar who authored several books. In one of his books he narrates a very interesting incident about a circus performer. In his act the performer would instantly subdue wild tigers freshly brought from the jungle. As soon as he would enter the tiger's cage and stare at the tiger, it would give up its aggressive behavior and start behaving like a pet kitten. This amazed everybody. Once Mahendranâth Datta asked the performer how he accomplished the feat. The man said, "A few minutes before entering the tiger's cage, I start thinking with great concentration that I am a tiger, only much bigger and more powerful than the one in the cage. Thinking intensely in this manner, when I enter the cage the tiger becomes subdued by my presence and starts behaving like a kitten." Mahendranâth Datta became curious and asked the performer if he would not mind demonstrating his technique. The performer agreed and sat in a chair. He shut his eyes and seemed to become absorbed in intense concentration. Within a few minutes his face started changing. It acquired a strange, ferocious look. The transformation was so abrupt and scary that Mahendranâth Datta became alarmed and asked the performer to stop whatever he was doing. Even after stopping, the performer took quite awhile to regain his usual mental composure.

This is an excellent example of what intense concentration or meditation can do for us. What we intensely think about, we eventually become. In other words, if we meditate on Divinity, we become Divinity.

Some lessons on meditation (Dhyâna)

During my stay in America for the past 27 years many have approached me for instruction in meditation. But some of the students I instructed did not take their spiritual practice seriously. They practiced for a short while and gave up. They gave up because they did not get quick results. They lacked patience and perseverance. It takes years of patient and steadfast effort to change the quality of the mind. A mind pampered through many years of sensual indulgence cannot be changed and controlled overnight. There is no instant success in spiritual life.

Once someone asked the famous inventor Thomas A. Edison, "Sir, what's the secret of your genius? Is it inspiration?"

Edison quickly replied, "It's 99% perspiration and only 1% inspiration!" This is all the more true for success in spiritual life. More than inspiration, it is the sustained hard labor of many years that helps one achieve success.

Those unsuccessful students may have had another reason for giving up meditation. In America there is a saying, "There's no such thing as a free lunch!" In other words, we cannot get anything worthwhile unless we pay for it! According to Hindu tradition, however, a spiritual teacher must never charge money for the instruction given. Following that sacred tradition I have never charged any money for the instructions I have given to students. Those who gave up the practice of meditation after trying for a short while might have thought that my instructions were of no value because they had been given to them for free! Had they practiced meditation for a longer period, they surely would have derived benefit from them.

Some lessons are given below that will give some idea about meditation. Students may practice one or more of these lessons and derive some benefit from them. But it is always better to have personal guidance from a proper teacher. Beyond the lessons given here, there are many more techniques of meditation. An experienced teacher knows what technique will suit which person. Besides, a student encounters many obstacles, even hazards, while practicing meditation. It may not be possible to overcome them without the help of an experienced teacher.

Where to meditate

Meditation is best done in a clean, quiet, and safe place. It should be a place where you will not be disturbed by anybody. If possible, have a separate room in your home for meditation. Nobody should be allowed to eat, drink, smoke, sleep or socialize there. The room should be free from all street and household noises—particularly those generated by phones and other noisy household appliances. If the room has a beautiful view, it can help your mind calm down before you meditate.

Avoid a damp, musty or malodorous room. A dry and well-ventilated room is preferable. During meditation your breathing will slow down and you will need more oxygen when you breathe. Decorate the walls of the room with inspirational pictures of saints, prophets, churches, temples and holy places. To deodorize the room you may use fragrant flowers or, if you are not allergic to smoke, burn a mildly fragrant incense stick (joss stick) while meditating.

If you cannot fulfill the above conditions, what should you do? Should you give up meditation? Certainly not. Regardless of the circumstances you should try to meditate. The advantage of having ideal conditions is that they make the practice of meditation easier. In less than perfect conditions you will find it harder to calm down the mind and concentrate.

What is the best time for meditation?

According to the sages of India, the best times to meditate are when night changes into day and day changes into night. In other words, sunrise and sunset hours are the best times for meditation. Yogîs have observed that around sunrise and sunset the mind naturally becomes calm and serene. A calm and serene mind is most conducive to meditation.[2] Nevertheless, if you have difficulty meditating at those hours, you may meditate whenever convenient. But you should try to meditate at the same time every day.

---

2. Yogîs also consider noon and midnight suitable for meditation. Many all-renouncing monks and Yogis meditate at noon and in the stillness of the midnight hours. However, these times may not be suitable for those who have to work for a living. Meditating at midnight is difficult for most people because they may feel sleepy.

Words of caution

Do not practice meditation when you are ill or when your body feels very lazy and tired. Nor should you meditate when your mind is extremely upset or grief-stricken. Avoid meditation when you are hungry. In all these situations it is hard to concentrate your mind.

Nor should you meditate with a full stomach because it will impair your digestion. After a heavy meal there is more blood circulation in the stomach to assist digestion. Meditation done at that time will cause more blood to circulate in the brain, depriving the stomach of its blood supply. It will also be hard for you to meditate after a big meal because you will feel sleepy. Ideally, your stomach should at least be half-empty when you meditate.

Try not to associate with too many people with secular interests. This will distract your mind. Too much talking also distracts the mind. Try to minimize unnecessary talking as much as possible. If you want to meditate, do not get involved in intense physical activity. Too much physical activity increases Rajas[3] and makes the mind restless. It will then be hard for you to control your mind and meditate.

Avoid sleeping too much or too little. Usually six hours of restful sleep should be adequate for most people, although some may need more. When you master the art of meditation you will be able to manage with fewer hours of sleep. Deep meditation gives the body and mind much more rest than sleep.

---

3. See the characteristics of Rajas on page 55.

Be careful about what you eat or drink. Drinks containing alcohol should be avoided, as also narcotics. Take only food that is easily assimilated and soothing to your constitution. Drink plenty of water to flush your system. It is not obligatory to become a vegetarian. Whether you are a vegetarian or a non-vegetarian, you have to practice moderation in your food habits. In either case overeating should be avoided, so also too much fasting. Unless you are allergic to dairy products, a diet consisting of milk, yogurt, cereals, fruits and vegetables is preferable. Eat only when your stomach is empty. Avoid eating between meals.

These instructions are for those who want to progress fast in the practice of Yoga. But for those who are busy earning their livelihood and can spend only a very short time on their daily meditation, moderation is the key word. They should practice moderation in whatever they do.

Preparation for meditation

If possible, take a shower before meditation. The shower will refresh your nerves and relax your body. Put on fresh clothes that are not tight fitting. Depending upon the season or the weather you may use either cooler or warmer clothes.

Sit in a straight-back wooden armchair with lumbar support. Your backbone should be kept erect and your head and neck held vertically in a straight line. Rest your elbows on the arms of the chair. Put your hands, loosely clasping each other, on your abdomen or lap. Avoid sitting in a metallic chair. It may drain out some of your body electricity. If you have to sit in one, cover it first with a woolen blanket or some other non-conducting material.

The other alternative is to sit cross-legged and meditate on a prayer rug placed on the floor. The rug should be of non-conducting material, such as wool. Sitting for meditation on a bare floor—be that of mud, cement or marble— is not advisable.

How to start your meditation

First salute your spiritual teacher, the sages and prophets of your religion, and God. Pray for their help to succeed in your practice of Yoga.

Meditations according to Râja Yoga

First meditation

Start breathing normally. Do not breathe hard. When breathing in, think that you are drawing in goodness, health and peace. When breathing out, think that you are letting out all your defects.

Second meditation

Shut your eyes. Think that there is a bright light in the region of your heart. Also think that your body is transparent. The light inside you is the light of selfless love. Think that this light is reaching out everywhere and gladdening the heart of everyone in the world.

Third meditation

Shut your eyes. "Imagine a lotus upon the top of your head, several inches up, with virtue as its center, and knowledge as its stalk. The eight petals of the lotus are the eight (supernatural) powers of the Yogî.[4] Inside, the stamens and pistils are renunciation. If the Yogî refuses the

---

4. See page 119 to know about the eight supernatural powers.

external powers he will come to salvation. So the petals of the lotus are the eight powers, but the internal stamens and pistils are extreme renunciation, the renunciation of all these powers. Inside of the lotus think of the Golden One, the Almighty, the Intangible, He whose name is Om (God), the Inexpressible, surrounded with effulgent light. Meditate on that."[5]

Fourth meditation

Shut your eyes. "Think of a space in your heart, and in the midst of that space think that a flame is burning steadily. Think of that flame as your own soul. Inside the flame is another effulgent light, and that is the Soul of your soul, God. Meditate upon that in the heart."[6]

Meditation according to Bhakti Yoga

Shut your eyes. Think that you are sitting in front of God, a Deity, or a Divine Incarnation. Think that a soothing light is being emitted by the body of the Deity or the Divine Incarnation. With your imagination try to create a vivid picture of the Deity or the Divine Incarnation. Think of the Deity or the Divine Incarnation as the personification of unconditional love and compassion. Think of yourself as a true child of God and the recipient of God's unconditional love.

If you are fond of the formless aspect of God then think of God as Divine radiance full of love and compassion.

---

5. Swâmî Vivekânanda, *Râja Yoga* (New York: Râmakrishna-Vivekânanda Center of N. Y., 1982), 91.
6. Ibid., 91-92.

Meditation according to Jnâna Yoga

Shut your eyes. Make the following affirmation: I am not the body or the mind. Nor am I the vital energy or the senses. I have no aversion nor clinging, greed, envy or false pride. I am not virtue or vice. Nothing mundane affects me. No impurity can touch me. I am the ever-pure Divine Spirit. I am birthless and deathless. I am ever free and one with Impersonal Divinity, Perfect Knowledge and Bliss. I am the Infinite and Eternal Spirit.

General points about all meditation techniques

To derive the maximum benefit from all these meditation techniques, you must not abruptly leave your seat after meditation. You should sit quietly for fifteen minutes to half an hour before starting your secular activities.

Judging by a student's temperament a teacher will decide which of the above meditations is suitable for the student, and give instructions accordingly. The student is not expected to practice all the techniques.

XI

OBSTACLES TO MEDITATION

Obstacles mentioned in Vedântasâra

According to *Vedântasâra*, a well-known book on non-dualistic Hindu philosophy, four obstacles are encountered when meditating:[1]

1. Sleep (Laya)

Sometimes one falls asleep while trying to meditate. This sleep, called Laya in Sanskrit, is an obstacle to meditation. Meditation is intense concentration, and if the mind is not under control, it is hard to concentrate. An uncontrolled mind naturally resents being controlled, and when one forcibly tries to concentrate the mind, one falls asleep. This is Laya.

Laya is a very restful and refreshing sleep, and those not experienced in meditation may consider it some kind of spiritual experience. Once a student of one of our Swâmîs in Europe came to him and announced proudly, "Swâmî, when I was meditating last night I experienced Samâdhi. I felt great inner peace!" On inquiry the Swâmî understood that the student had not had Samâdhi. Instead, he had

---

1. *Vedântasâra* by Sadananda Yogîndra, Para. 82.

encountered the obstacle Laya. When the Swâmî explained that to the student, he did not like it. He left the Swâmî and went to some other teacher.

Laya is caused by a temporary preponderance of Tamas[2] in the mind. To prevent Laya it is best to meditate when not tired. A tired body naturally induces Laya. At the end of a busy working day one may easily feel tired and may fall asleep during meditation. Early morning is more suitable for meditation because the mind and body are fresh and alert at that time. If one wants to meditate in the evening it is advisable to have an afternoon nap, if possible, for one hour. This will effectively prevent sleepiness during meditation. Sleeping longer than one hour may produce an adverse effect. It may make the body and mind sluggish and lethargic.

2. Wandering of the mind (Vikshepa)

One may occasionally find it very hard to meditate because the mind keeps wandering. This restless wandering of mind is called Vikshepa in Sanskrit. It is the second major obstacle to meditation. This obstacle appears when the mind has a preponderance of Rajas.[3]

Usually two techniques are used to overcome this obstacle. The first is to force the mind by sheer will power to concentrate on the object of meditation. A person who lacks adequate will power will find it hard to do. It may also pose a health hazard for someone suffering from hypertension by temporarily raising the blood pressure.

---

2. See page 55 to know about Tamas.
3. See page 55 to know about Rajas.

In the second technique one says to the wandering mind, "Go wherever you want, but know that I'll be watching you." As one watches the mind, it stops wandering and gradually becomes calm. This entire process usually takes ten or fifteen minutes, though for some it may take longer. Once the mind has been made calm it can be focused on its object of meditation.

3. Reluctançe to practice meditation (Kashâya)

The third obstacle, Kashâya, is a feeling of intense reluctance to practice meditation. At that time meditation appears to be extremely dry and tasteless. This obstacle is caused by past thoughts or Samskâras[4] lying latent in the mind. No thought is ever lost. All past thoughts are stored in the subconscious level of the mind. They lie there like so many seeds. Just as every seed retains the characteristics of its parent plant, so also these seed thoughts or Samskâras retain the characteristics of their full-blown conscious state. Some were holy and pious thoughts, some vulgar, some loving, some violent. Innumerable thoughts of diverse tendencies are stored in the subconscious level, and each one—borrowing a mathematical term—can be called a vector. The resultant mental condition of these countless vectors is Kashâya. The mind in this state is neither sleepy nor restless as in Laya or Vikshepa. It lacks any recognizable thought pattern other than an intense lack of interest in meditation. It can aptly be described as a state of mental drought.

To counteract this obstacle any of the following can be helpful: (i) Singing devotional songs or listening to devo-

---

4. See page 57 to know more about Samskâras.

tional music; (ii) Reading inspirational religious literature; (iii) Imagining giving personal service to God, a Divine Incarnation, or a prophet. This type of imagining is called Lîlâ-Dhyâna in Hinduism. Any of these techniques is capable of removing the feeling of dryness from the mind. It should be noted, however, that one must not leave one's seat while practicing these techniques. As soon as the mental dryness is gone one must start meditating.

4. *Getting stuck in an intermediate joyful spiritual experience (Rasâ-Swâda)*

The fourth obstacle, Rasâ-Swâda, literally means tasting something sweet and flavorful. This obstacle is encountered after the meditator has made considerable spiritual progress through meditation and yet not reached the goal. The meditator has grown fond of the taste of some intermediate joyful spiritual experiences, has become stuck there and does not want to progress further and strive for God-vision. Needless to say, one should overcome this obstacle. Otherwise, one will deprive oneself of the highest spiritual experience. Shrî Râmakrishna tells the following beautiful parable to stress this point:

> Once upon a time a woodcutter went into a forest to collect wood. There, by chance, he met a holy man. The holy man said to him, "My good man, go forward." So saying the holy man went away.
>
> On returning home the woodcutter asked himself, "Why did the holy man tell me to go forward?" Some time passed. One day he remembered the holy man's words. He said to himself, "Today I shall go deeper into the forest." Going deep into the forest, he discovered innumerable sandalwood trees. He was very happy and returned with cart-

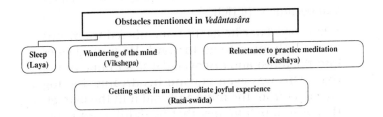

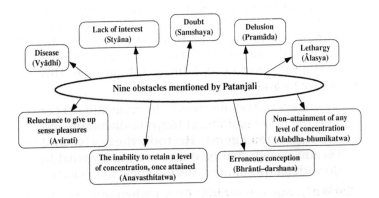

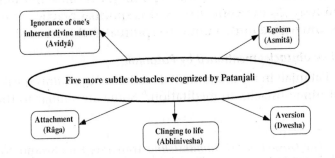

loads of sandalwood. He sold them in the market and became very rich.

A few days later he again remembered the words of the holy man to go forward. He went deeper into the forest and discovered a silver mine near a river. This was even beyond his dreams. He dug out silver from the mine and sold it in the market. He got so much money that he didn't even know how much he had.

A few more days passed. One day he thought: "The holy man didn't ask me to stop at the silver mine, he told me to go forward." This time he went to the other side of the river and found a gold mine. Then he exclaimed: "Ah, just see! This is why he asked me to go forward."

Again, a few days afterwards, he went still deeper into the forest and found heaps of diamonds and other precious gems. He took these also and became so rich that he didn't even know what to do with all this money! His joy knew no bounds.[5]

Similarly, one will get infinite joy when one experiences God at the end of the spiritual journey. One must not stop midway. To overcome Rasâ-Swâda spiritual practice must be intensified further until the spiritual goal is reached.

Nine obstacles mentioned by Patanjali

Patanjali in his monumental work the *Yoga-Sûtras* speaks of nine obstacles to meditation.[6] Some are similar to the

---

5. *The Gospel of Sri Ramakrishna* translated by Swâmî Nikhilânanda (New York: Ramakrishna-Vivekananda Center of N.Y., 1942), 453-54.
6. *Yoga-Sûtras*, 1/30.

obstacles mentioned in *Vedântasâra*. These obstacles may come in the form of the following disturbances:

1. Disease (Vyâdhi)

An ordinary person's body and mind are closely intertwined. If anything happens to the body, the mind becomes affected. When the body becomes diseased, the mind also gets disturbed. A disturbed mind cannot meditate. Most diseases can be prevented by a healthy lifestyle—a life of moderation. Nevertheless, if diseases come, one should seek the help of qualified physicians to cure them.

2. Lack of interest (Styâna)

Sometimes one may suffer from lack of interest in the practice of meditation. No matter how difficult or unpleasant it may be, according to some Yogîs only steadfast and relentless effort made with great vigor can overcome this obstacle.

3. Doubt (Samshaya)

Doubts about the efficacy of meditation or even about its goal may come occasionally. This will happen as long as one has not derived any genuine spiritual experience from meditation, such as clairvoyance (the ability to see what is happening far away), clairaudience (the power to hear what people are saying beyond one's range of hearing), etc. These experiences strengthen one's faith by removing doubts, and inspire one to persevere.[7] Unfortunately, it takes many years of spiritual practice to gain such experiences. One cannot have them overnight. The

---

7. Ibid., 1/33.

inspiration received from the company of one's Guru or other genuine holy men can also effectively dispel such doubts. In addition, one should also think: "The illumined sages—whose lives were established in truthfulness—have vouched for the efficacy of these spiritual techniques. These selfless souls didn't care for name, fame, power or position. All that they wanted was the well-being of mankind. They had no reason to lie. It is also true that many have attained spiritual illumination by following these techniques. Why don't I give these techniques a try and see what happens!" This kind of thinking can be of immense help in eliminating doubts.

In some forms of psychosis, patients imagine that they can hear what people are saying about them at a great distance. They also have the illusion that they are able to see events happening many miles away, or they may see strange lights. People not knowledgeable about Yoga may erroneously consider these as signs of spiritual progress, but Yogîs know them to be nothing but hallucinations. Hallucinations make people lose touch with reality while genuine Yogic experiences and visions help them come closer to the Divine Reality.

4. Delusion (Pramâda)

Here *Pramâda* or delusion has a special meaning. It means failing to think about engaging in the different techniques of concentration that lead to Samâdhi. A deluded mind gets involved in harmful worldly pursuits, forgetting the benefits of meditation and other helpful spiritual disciplines. Or worse, some may imagine that they have made great spiritual progress while they have not made any.

5. Lethargy (Âlasya)

This obstacle manifests itself as physical and mental heaviness or lethargy and is caused by the preponderance of Tamas. Lethargy makes one unwilling to meditate. One's mind becomes torpid.[8] It can be shaken off by sustained and determined effort. In addition, a diet that helps one feel light-bodied and alert can be useful in overcoming this obstacle.

6. Reluctance to give up sense pleasures (Avirati)

Attachment to objects of sense pleasure is a great obstacle to meditation. Such attachment causes the tendency not to give up sense pleasures (Avirati). Meditators have to wean themselves away from sense pleasures to overcome this obstacle. This can be done by recognizing the defects in sense pleasures. For instance, someone addicted to liquor may succeed in giving up the addiction only after really being able to see the defects of alcoholism. In addition, according to Patanjali, meditation on the pure heart of a holy person who has gone beyond attachment to sense objects can help one to overcome this obstacle, because what one thinks with great concentration, that one eventually becomes.[9]

7. Erroneous conception (Bhrânti-darshana)

Erroneous conception is false knowledge. Not knowing clearly which allurements should be given up to enhance spiritual progress, or not knowing clearly how to give up such allurements, is called erroneous conception. Mistaking what is harmful to spiritual life as beneficial, and what

---

8. Ibid., 1/30
9. Ibid., 1/37.

is spiritually beneficial as harmful, is also false knowledge. Such erroneous thinking is undoubtedly an obstacle to Yoga.

8. Non-attainment of any level of concentration (Alabdha-bhûmikatwa)

The capacity for concentration comes in stages. *Alabdha-bhûmikatwa* or the inability to attain any level of concentration is an obstacle. To overcome this obstacle one should steadfastly follow the meditative process until a valid level of concentration is achieved. After attaining the first level one should strive for higher levels of concentration.

9. Inability to retain a level of concentration once attained (Anavasthitatwa)

Even after reaching a level of concentration it is possible for one to slide down. This inability to retain a certain level of concentration is called Anavasthitatwa. To overcome this one must further intensify one's practice of meditation. Perseverance is the key to overcoming this obstacle.

Five more subtle obstacles recognized by Patanjali

The following five obstacles[10] are more subtle and deep-rooted than those mentioned above. These are called Kleshah or pain-bearing obstructions.

1. Ignorance of one's inherent divine nature (Avidyâ)

Divinity must be equally present in every thing and every being. If not, it contradicts God's omnipresence. But

---

10. Ibid., 2/3.

divinity, though equally present, is not equally manifest in every being. What obstructs this manifestation is Avidyâ. Ignorance of our inherent divinity is Avidyâ. Like a dense cloud Avidyâ does not allow us to see the Sun of divinity within. Instead, it makes us think, "I am the body-mind-complex, and not the pure, effulgent and ever-blissful Divine Self." This kind of confused thinking is caused by delusion. This great delusion is Avidyâ. It is the cause of egoism (Asmitâ), attachment (Râga), aversion (Dwesha) and blind clinging to life (Abhinivesha). Avidyâ can only be eliminated by the experiential knowledge of our inherent divinity. This knowledge can be attained through Samâdhi, the most mature state of meditation.

2. Egoism (Asmitâ)

Egoism causes false identification with our body-mind complex. Due to Avidyâ or ignorance we become oblivious of our eternal, ever perfect and immutable Divine Self and falsely identify with the body, mind, energy, and senses—which are non-eternal and subject to constant change. Owing to this false identification we sometimes say, "I am happy," or "I am angry." Happiness and anger are mental states only. It is the mind that becomes happy or angry, not the Self. Our changeless Divine Self is always the same. How can it be happy or angry? This false identification of the Self with the non-Self is egoism (Asmitâ). It is caused by the ignorance of our true Divine Self. In Sanskrit this ignorance is called Avidyâ. The true knowledge of the inherent Divine Self will overcome egoism or Asmitâ.

3. Attachment (Râga)

Attachment or Râga is clinging to whatever is pleasurable. Such clinging binds the mind down to matter—the sense objects of the world. This prevents the realization of the indwelling Divine Spirit.

4. Aversion (Dwesha)

Aversion or Dwesha is the urge to get away from whatever is painful. According to Vyâsa,[11] aversion is also the feeling of opposition, the propensity to hurt out of anger and malice the objects or persons causing pain, or to hate suffering itself. Such urges are created by the recollection of the suffering experienced before.

Aversion may seem to be the opposite of attachment, yet they are two sides of the same coin. Attachment (Râga) and aversion (Dwesha) follow each other in a cyclic order. Aversion leads to attachment and attachment leads to aversion. An analogy will make this idea clear. Suppose a boy is extremely fond of chocolate cupcakes. If at gunpoint he is forced to eat eight cupcakes in quick succession, eating the first cupcake will be a delight, but eating the eighth one will be a torture. As a result, his attachment to cupcakes will be transformed, at least for a while, into aversion.

Aversion to pain also urges us to seek out and cling to what is pleasant. In this manner, aversion causes attachment—which in turn hinders our experiencing the indwelling Divine Self.

---

11. Vyâsa, an illustrious Hindu sage of ancient India, was the compiler of the Vedas. He also wrote a commentary on the *Yoga-Sûtras* of Patanjali. This reference is to that commentary.

Patanjali says that if we wish to counteract hatred or malice we should be friendly and compassionate to all. We should be happy at the happiness of others and sympathetic to those in distress. We should not be obsessed with finding faults in others. We should try to ignore the faults of others by thinking that everyone—no matter how bad—must have some good qualities also. The world appears to be dark and dismal to those who see only the dark sides of people. On the other hand, the world appears to be full of goodness to those who see goodness in others. Depressing and negative thoughts should be eliminated through the practice of indifference (Upekshâ). These practices will make the mind calm and peaceful.[12]

The indifference mentioned above does not mean playing a passive role and condoning evil and injustice in the world. One must try to minimize them through effective but humanitarian means. What Patanjali means by the practice of indifference is learning to put up with the unpleasant reality of this less-than-perfect world by being detached from some of its chronic problems—problems that are extremely deep-rooted. Disparity of privileges is one such chronic problem. Most problems in the world are social evils rooted in the selfishness of people. It is selfishness which makes people evil. Had it been possible to transform them into perfect human beings by wiping out their selfishness, the world would have become perfect.

But is it possible for anyone like me to create such a perfect world? As others are not under my control, it is not

---

12. Maitrî-karunâ-mudito-pekshânâm sukha-duhkha-punyâ-punya-vishayânâm bhâvanâ-tashchitta-prasâdanam—*Yoga-Sûtras*, 1/33.

possible for me to transform others and make them perfect. On the other hand, there is one person who is under my control—whom I can transform and make perfect. That person is no other than myself. If I can make myself perfect, to that extent the world will also be perfect. Rather than being an obsessed do-gooder, I should try to change myself first before trying to change the world.

In this context it should be clearly understood that the above instructions given by Patanjali are meant only for those keen on experiencing God. Those who have not developed that kind of yearning should surely try to do good to the world by giving whatever service they deem fit.

5. Clinging to life (Abhinivesha)

Instinctive and obsessive clinging to the body—the unrealistic yearning to perpetuate the existence of the body for a long time, if not forever—is called Abhinivesha. Such clinging is a great obstacle to experiencing the pure, perfect and ever-blissful nature of the soul or Divine Self. We should realize the inevitability of death and be mentally prepared for it. We should even meditate on it. Buddhism teaches its adherents to meditate on the inevitability of death and the transitoriness of the world. There is a story from India in which we find a beautiful example of Abhinivesha—this blind clinging to life.

In a certain village there lived a very old woman. She was extremely poor and had become very feeble from old age. She had no family, and made a meager living by collecting windfalls from the forest—twigs and branches—and selling them in her village.

One day a big storm knocked down the branches of many trees in the forest. When the storm subsided, the woman went to the forest and was exceedingly glad to see so many windfalls lying all around. With great effort she made a huge bundle of the twigs and branches and said to herself joyfully, "At last God has smiled upon me! I'll be able to sell this wood at a good price in my village. Then I'll come again and again and carry the rest of this wood to my village." So saying, she tried to put the bundle on her back and carry it to her village. She tried many times, but failed because the bundle was too heavy. This made her extremely upset. Totally disgusted with life, she cried out, "O Yama,[13] king of death, where are you? Take me away from this wretched world. I don't want to live here anymore!"

Immediately Yama appeared before the startled woman and said, "You called me; so I've come to take you to the other world."

"No, Yama, that's not why I called you!" protested the woman, "I need your help. I called you to put this bundle on my back. I don't want to go with you yet."

To overcome Abhinivesha we should not be suicidal or careless about the body. Committing suicide is strictly forbidden by the Hindu scriptures. As long as the body lasts it should be taken care of and put to good use. And the greatest good comes to those who fruitfully utilize their lives by striving for spiritual enlightenment.

---

13. According to Hindu mythology Yama is the king of death. This should not be confused with the other meaning of the word: restraining harmful thoughts and impulses.

In the West, thinking of death is considered morbid and is strongly discouraged. At the same time, developing a realistic attitude towards life is highly encouraged. But if we are realists we should recognize both life and death as facts. To think that we can avoid death by simply ignoring it is not realistic. It is escapism. If we recognize death as an inevitable reality, we are more likely to use this precious life more fruitfully and constructively.

Other obstacles experienced by spiritual aspirants

1. Temptation

In the lives of Gautama Buddha, Jesus Christ and Shrî Râmakrishna we read about another obstacle. This obstacle is temptation.

According to Buddhist mythology Buddha was tempted by Mâra (the evil entity), who wanted to give Buddha sensual pleasures, wealth, honor, power, etc. But Buddha declined the offer. The New Testament tells us that the devil took Jesus to a very high mountain and showed him all the great kingdoms of the world. Then the devil offered him those kingdoms on condition that Jesus worship the devil as his Lord. Jesus did not succumb to this temptation. Pâpapurusha (the personification of sin) wanted to tempt Shrî Râmakrishna by offering him sense pleasure, wealth, etc., but he did not yield to the temptation.

2. Intense fear (Bhaya-bhairava)

The Buddhist tradition mentions an obstacle, Bhaya-Bhairava, a feeling of intense fear experienced by some who have made considerable spiritual progress. Such fear can dissuade the spiritual aspirants from their spiritual path. According to Hinduism, these obstacles are only created by the spiritual aspirant's mind.

Four physical and mental disturbances caused by an unconcentrated mind

A concentrated mind is calm, serene and immune to any mental or physical disturbances. But, according to Patanjali, an unconcentrated or distracted mind causes the following four mental and physical disturbances:[14]

1. Grief (Duhkha)

According to Hindu tradition, grief or Duhkha is of three kinds. The first kind—Âdhyâtmika-duhkha—arises on its own in the mind. The second kind—Âdhibhautika-duhkha—is inflicted by other people or creatures, such as injuries caused by other human beings or animals. The third kind—Âdhidaivika-duhkha—is caused by natural calamities or acts of God, such as earthquakes, devastating floods, etc. All three disturb meditation.

According to Patanjali, one who meditates on the Effulgent Light in the region of one's heart gets rid of grief.[15] Also an intense thought of compassion can counteract grief.[16] When the mind has a preponderance of Sattwa-Guna it is full of joy and peace. Duhkha or grief indicates that the mind does not have a preponderance of Sattwa-Guna. Either meditation on the Effulgent Light in the heart or an intense thought of compassion causes Sattwa-Guna to become preponderant in the mind. Thus, grief is overcome.

---

14. *Yoga-Sûtras*, 1/31.
15. Ibid., 1/36.
16. Ibid., 1/33.

2. Despair (Daurmanasya)

Despair is caused by disappointment at not having one's expectations fulfilled. One should minimize expectations to prevent despair. •

3. Involuntary nervous trembling of the body
   (Anga-mejayatwa)

If someone who does not usually become angry becomes terribly angry after intense provocation, that person's body may start shaking involuntarily. Such shaking is a nervous reaction to the anger. If the same person frequently becomes angry, that person's nerves will get used to such outbursts of anger and the body will not shake. So also with the practice of concentration; one may experience involuntary nervous shaking when one newly practices concentration. In course of time when one is able to meditate properly, such trembling will disappear. Proper concentration will bring perfect repose to one's body and mind every time one practices meditation. When one's mind is concentrated and calm, one will not have such nervous shaking.

4. Irregular breathing (Shwâsa-prashwâsa-vikshepa)

When the mind lacks control and concentration, it can be swayed by fluctuating moods, causing irregular breathing. The practice of rhythmic or regulated breathing under the guidance of a competent teacher enables a meditator to overcome irregular breathing.

XII

HAZARDS IN MEDITATION

Besides the obstacles mentioned in the previous chapter, there are also hazards associated with meditation.

Dangers caused by the keen mind of an advanced student of meditation

Through the practice of Japa and meditation our minds gradually become sharper. We gain greater control over our minds and become capable of deeper concentration. A highly concentrated mind can be compared to a laser beam. A laser beam is a highly concentrated flow of photons. Such a beam can burn holes even in the hardest steel. Ordinary dissipated light cannot do that. Similarly, the thoughts of a highly concentrated mind are much more powerful than those of a scattered mind. If such thoughts are good, they can be very beneficial. If they are bad they can do immense harm. The angry or lustful thoughts of a concentrated mind can do much more harm than the thoughts of a scattered mind. For that reason, if we have gained some degree of concentration, we should carefully avoid harmful and negative thoughts. Otherwise, those negative thoughts can do immense harm to both ourselves and others.

I knew a young man in India who was not married and wanted to lead the life of a celibate monk. He left home and went to a holy place in the Himalayas to perform spiritual austerities. He lived there for three or four years practicing Japa and meditation for many hours a day. Consequently, he developed a very sharp mind. One night a lustful thought came to his mind. The thought was so overwhelming and stubborn that no matter how much he tried he could not shake it off. Unfortunately, he did not have a proper spiritual teacher. Nor did he belong to a monastic order. In this predicament his teacher could have come to his rescue, or the monastic environment could have given him much-needed protection. But he did not have such help. As a result, he returned home and married shortly thereafter.

He did not have a college education and was unable to find a well-paying job. Holding a low-paying position, he had to work very hard to make a living. There was hardly any time or energy left for spiritual practice. During one of my visits to India he came to see me and told me his sad story. His life is an example of how hazards in meditation can harm a person's spiritual life.

The danger of being critical of others

The keen mind of a meditator is an incisive mind. With its help the meditator can easily probe into his or her own mind, discover its hidden defects and eliminate them. How the mind can cleanse itself can be explained using the analogy of a vacuum cleaner. A vacuum cleaner has an attachment meant for cleaning hardwood floors. The attachment has a brush at its cleaning end. While vacuuming, the brush often collects a lot of lint. How can this brush be cleaned? To clean the brush, the attachment must first be taken off. Then the same vacuum cleaner is used to suck in the collected lint from the brush. Similarly, using our own concentrated minds we can gradually cleanse our minds of all defects and impurities.

But a mind sharpened by meditation acquires the ability to see other people's defects as well. If we want to reach the goal of our spiritual life faster, we should develop the habit of not seeing other people's defects. Otherwise, we may face the hazard of becoming overcritical of others. Shrî Râmakrishna used to say that the mind is like a piece of white cloth. It takes on the color of any dye in which it is soaked. If the mind dwells on other people's defects it becomes impure by absorbing them. Meditators should avoid this hazard by not being critical of others.

Craving praise & appreciation can be a hazard

Craving praise can be a hazard in spiritual life. This desire is expressed in many devious ways. One expression is gossip. Gossip is indirect self-praise. If we can prove through gossip that all others are bad, then we have indirectly proved that we are better. This false sense of superiority harms us by obstructing our further spiritual growth.

Psychologists speak of a universal dream in which dreamers see themselves flying through the air. One characteristic of this dream is that the dreamers alone can fly—others cannot. This gives dreamers a sense of greater power and makes them feel superior to others. In the real world for various reasons they may feel inferior. They want to compensate for that deficiency by feeling superior to others in their dreams. This same kind of thinking encourages people to indulge in gossiping.

In the presence of others some have the habit of glorifying their spiritual teachers. Such glorification is often a ploy to indirectly exalt themselves. For example, if a disciple claims his or her Guru to be a Divine Incarnation, then he or she is automatically raised to the elevated position of an apostle! This distinction is achieved without having to go through any rigorous spiritual discipline!

Sometimes self-glorification is accomplished in a very subtle way. Once in India I overheard an interesting conversation between two persons belonging to a certain religious group. One was in his sixties and the other person was about thirty. The older person asked the younger man, "Do you have a Guru?"

"Yes, sir," replied the young man.

"May I know his name?" asked the older person. In reply, the young man mentioned the name of a well-known Indian saint who was no longer alive.

Thereupon the older person said, "I'm also his disciple. Isn't it interesting that both of us are disciples of the same Guru?" Then he asked, "May I know when you became his disciple?"

The young man mentioned a certain year. Hearing that, the older person said, "I see! Around that period he had become very liberal; just about anyone approaching him could become his disciple! I became his disciple a long time before that. When I became his disciple he was very picky and choosy. At that time he would not accept anybody and everybody as his disciple."

The craving for praise and appreciation often brings disappointment and depression. One problem inherent in this kind of desire is that its satisfaction depends entirely upon the whims of others. As others are under no obligation to offer praise and appreciation, one who craves such attention is bound to be disappointed at one time or the other. Depending upon the intensity of the craving, such disappointments may cause anger or severe depression.

The hazards of supernatural powers gained through the practice of meditation

The Hindu scriptures speak of eight supernatural powers that come to spiritual aspirants in course of their spiritual progress. Each power is called a Siddhi in Sanskrit. They are as follows:

1. The ability to become as small as a molecule and penetrate solid objects (Animâ)
2. Extreme lightness of body or the ability to levitate (Laghimâ)
3. The ability to permeate everything (Vyâpti)
4. The acquisition of irresistible will power (Prâkâmya)
5. The ability to make the body extremely large (Mahimâ)
6. Acquiring godlike powers (Îshitwa)
7. The power to bring everything under one's control (Vashitwa)
8. The ability to obtain whatever one desires (Kâma-vasâyitâ)

The *Uddhava Gîtâ*,[1] however, describes the Siddhis as follows:

1. The power to overcome hunger and thirst (Anurmi-mattwam)
2. The ability to hear what is being said far away (Dûra-shravanam)
3. The power to see what is happening far away (Dûra-darshanam)
4. The ability to move the body as fast as the speed of the mind (Mano-javitwam)
5. The ability to transform the body into any other desired physical form (Kâma-rûpam)
6. The power to enter the body of any other person (Para-kâya-praveshanam)
7. The power to die at will (Swechchhâ-mrityuh) [This should not, however, be confused with committing suicide, which is condemned by the Hindu scriptures.]
8. The ability to enjoy the celestial pleasures of the gods or angels (Deva-krîdânudarshanam)
9. The ability to fulfill one's desires (Yathâ-samkalpa-samsiddhi)
10. The ability to order other people to do things without any opposition from them (Âjnâ-apratihata)
11. The ability to know the past, present and future (Trikâlajnatwam)
12. The ability to read the thoughts of others (Parachittâdi-abhijnatâ)
13. The power not to be affected by fire, water and poison (Agni-arka-vishâdinâm pratishtambha)

---

1. *Uddhava Gîtâ*. 10/6–8

14. The ability to remain undefeated under any
circumstances (Aparâjaya)

Other supernatural powers may also come to the Yogî:

1. The power to fly (Khecharî-vidyâ)
2. The power to conquer death (Mrityunjaya-
vidyâ)
3. The ability to acquire treasures hidden under-
ground (Pâtâla-siddhi)
4. The power to make oneself invisible
(Antardhânam)
5. The power to understand all animal languages
(Sarvabhûtaruta-jnânam)
6. Acquiring the knowledge of past lives (Pûrvajâti-jnânam)

The readers may think that such supernatural powers
are impossible to attain. Some may even dismiss them as
cock-and-bull stories. But the lives of genuine saints,
prophets and godmen belonging to all religions bear testi-
mony to the validity of these claims. Such powers can
only be attained through intense concentration and many
years of steady and relentless spiritual practice. The acquisition of one or more of these powers initially generates
enthusiasm in spiritual aspirants to continue with their
practice. But once attained, these powers should not be
misused or used prematurely before attaining spiritual
enlightenment. These powers or *Siddhis*, although
extremely attractive, are a great danger for spiritual aspirants. Lord Krishna, a Divine Incarnation, told his devotee
Uddhava that anyone who craves supernatural powers
cannot have God-vision.[2] Lord Buddha asked one of his

---

2. Ibid., 15/33.

close disciples not to use any Siddhis because that would be extremely detrimental to his spiritual life. Only people who have reached the goal of spiritual life know how to use these powers without harming themselves or others. For those who have not reached the goal, these powers are a great danger. Shrî Râmakrishna warns us of this hazard through the following parable:

An ascetic gained supernatural powers through his spiritual austerities. One day, while he was sitting on the bank of a big river, a severe storm arose. Using his supernatural power he instantly stopped the storm. At that moment a boat carrying a large number of passengers was going along in full sail on the river. When the storm stopped abruptly the boat's sails suddenly collapsed, and a huge following wave engulfed the boat and it instantly sank. Many passengers died. As a result, the ascetic lost all his supernatural powers. And when he died he went to hell for causing the death of all those people.

Before entering into a discussion on Samâdhi—the next higher step of concentration—it will be helpful for us to understand the concept of Kundalinî power in Râja Yoga. The next chapter deals with that subject.

XIII

KUNDALINÎ POWER AND
THE SIX CHAKRAS

According to Râja Yoga the spiritual power in humans, which usually remains dormant, is called Kundalinî. This word is derived from the Sanskrit word *Kundalî*, meaning a coil. Kundalinî means something that is in the shape of a coil. Like a coiled-up snake in a state of hibernation this Kundalinî power remains asleep near the lower extremity of our backbone. Through meditation and the other spiritual disciplines of Râja Yoga, we can awaken the Kundalinî.

According to Râja Yoga the human backbone has in it three extremely narrow channels. If we imagine the backbone or spinal column to be so many figure 8's piled one on top of the other, forming two vertical channels side by side, then the vital energy or nerve current of a person will work in the body by passing through these two channels. The left channel is called Idâ and the right channel Pingalâ. If a person's breath is stronger through the left nostril when exhaling, it is an indication that the vital energy is flowing through the Idâ channel. Similarly, if the outgoing breath is stronger through the right nostril, the energy is flowing through the Pingalâ channel. When a person is doing a lot of physical activity, energy flows through the

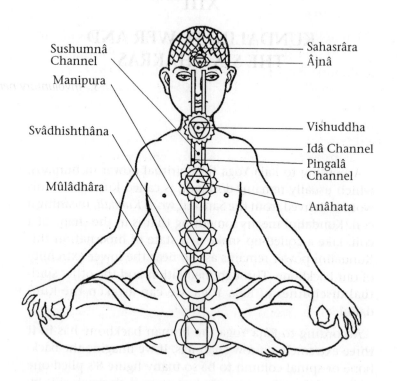

Sushumnâ Channel

Manipura

Svâdhishthâna

Mûlâdhâra

Sahasrâra

Âjnâ

Vishuddha

Idâ Channel

Pingalâ Channel

Anâhata

The Seven Chakras

Pingalâ channel. When resting, energy flows through the Idâ channel.

There is a third narrow channel between the Idâ and Pingalâ channels. Its name is Sushumnâ. Normally the Sushumnâ channel remains closed at the bottom. It opens up when the Kundalinî is awakened. The awakened Kundalinî begins coursing through the Sushumnâ channel towards the brain. When that happens, the spiritual aspirant enters into an altogether different domain of experience and starts having genuine spiritual experiences. When the awakened Kundalinî starts moving toward the brain, it seems to pass through different doors, each introducing the spiritual aspirant to a newer set of genuine spiritual experiences. Each door or level of spiritual experience is called a Chakra. Râja Yoga speaks of seven such levels, the topmost one of which is Sahasrâra. The Sahasrâra is located somewhere inside the brain. The lowest one, at the lower end of the spinal cord, is called Mûlâdhâra. The next higher Chakra is Swâdhishthâna, then in succession come Manipura, Anâhata, Vishuddha, Âjnâ, and Sahasrâra.

The scriptures say that the Chakras look like lotuses and can be mentally visualized by pure-minded Yogîs. Chakras, as described in the next paragraph, are not made of matter, energy, or mind. According to Shrî Râmakrishna, they are made of Divine Consciousness.

1. The lotus at the Mûlâdhâra Chakra—at the base of the spinal column—is a crimson colored lotus with four petals.
2. The Swâdhishthâna Chakra—located at the sacral plexus near the organ of reproduction—is a vermilion colored lotus with six petals.

3. The Manipura Chakra—at the level of the
    navel—is a grayish-blue lotus with ten petals.
4. The Anâhata Chakra—at the level of the
    heart—is a red lotus with twelve petals.
5. The Vishuddha Chakra—situated in the
    region of the throat—is a lotus with sixteen
    smoky purple petals.
6. The Âjnâ Chakra—lying between the eye-
    brows—is a white lotus with two petals.
7. The Sahasrâra Chakra—located at the top of
    the head—is a sparklingly white lotus with its
    head turned downward. It has one thousand
    petals.

In Hinduism we read about three types of space. The
space this physical universe occupies is called Mahâkâsha
or Outer Space. Our dreams, thoughts and imaginings
exist in Chittâkâsha or Mental Space. All genuine spiritual
experiences take place in Chidâkâsha or Knowledge Space.
We get access to Chidâkâsha only when our Kundalinî
power has awakened and entered into the Sushumnâ
channel.

All experiences in Mental Space (Chittâkâsha) are imagination or hallucinations compared to the genuine spiritual experiences of Knowledge Space (Chidâkâsha). When
the Kundalinî power courses through the Sushumnâ channel and reaches the Sahasrâra, we become spiritually illumined. We attain the goal of Yoga. The ascent of the
Kundalinî power to the Sahasrâra Chakra results in
Asamprajnâta Samâdhi. (Chapter XV will clearly explain
what this Samâdhi is.)

The Kundalinî power is also called Mahâvâyu or the
Great Energy. The ways the awakened Kundalinî power

courses through the Sushumnâ channel toward the Sahasrâra have been described by Shrî Râmakrishna from his
own experience. He described the five different ways the
Kundalinî power proceeds from the Mûlâdhâra Chakra to
the Sahasrâra Chakra:

> Just as a monkey climbs a tree, jumping from one
> branch to another, so also does the Mahâvâyu, the
> Great Energy, rise in the body, jumping from one
> center (Chakra) to another, and one goes into
> Samâdhi. One feels the rising of the Great Energy,
> as though it were the movement of a monkey.

> Just as a fish darts about in the water and roams in
> great happiness, so also does the Mahâvâyu move
> upward in the body, and one goes into Samâdhi.
> One feels the rising of the Great Energy, as though
> it were the movement of a fish.

> Like a bird hopping from one branch to another,
> the Mahâvâyu goes up in the tree of the body,
> now to this branch and now to that. One feels the
> rising of the Great Energy, as though it were the
> movement of a bird.

> Like the slow creeping of an ant, the Mahâvâyu
> rises from center (Chakra) to center (Chakra).
> When it reaches the Sahasrâra one goes into
> Samâdhi. One feels the rising of the Great Energy,
> as though it were the movement of an ant.

> Like the wriggling of a snake, the Mahâvâyu rises
> in a zigzag way along the spinal column till it
> reaches the Sahasrâra, and one goes into Samâdhi.
> One feels the rising of the Great Energy, as though
> it were the movement of a snake.[1]

Before discussing the last step of Patanjali's eight-step discipline for Yoga, it is necessary to have some knowledge of the theory of creation according to the Sânkhya school of Hindu philosophy.

1. *The Gospel of Sri Ramakrishna* translated from Bengali by Swâmî Nikhilânanda (New York: Ramakrishna-Vivekananda Center, 1942), 949-950.

XIV

THE SÂNKHYA THEORY OF CREATION

The Sânkhya system is the most ancient school of Hindu philosophy. This system recognizes two types of ultimate reality, Purusha and Prakriti. Purusha is pure consciousness or pure sentience. It is uncaused, changeless, eternal, all-pervading and totally devoid of matter. It is also entirely passive. Unlike Prakriti, which is only one, there are innumerable Purushas. There are as many Purushas as there are conscious beings.

Objections have been raised by other schools of Hindu philosophy about the Sânkhya concept of many Purushas. According to them, since Purusha is all-pervading, the idea of many Purushas occupying the same space is not acceptable. The Sânkhya reply to this objection is that Purushas have no difficulty co-existing, just as light from different candles can occupy the same space without any conflict.

Prakriti is unconscious primordial matter. It is uncaused. Though Prakriti is uncaused, it is the cause of everything in this universe, whether matter, energy or even mind. Hindu psychology very clearly states that mind, however

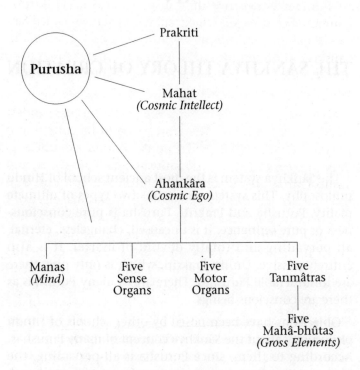

Creation according to Sânkhya Philosophy

subtle, is a material substance. It also should be remembered that although Prakriti is the cause of everything in this universe, it is not the cause of Purusha. Prakriti is composed of three extremely subtle substances called Sattwa, Rajas and Tamas. Each substance is called a Guna in Sanskrit. Although the characteristics of these Gunas have already been discussed in a preceding chapter,[1] it is worthwhile recapitulating them in the context of creation.

According to Sânkhya philosophy, Prakriti is the subtlest of all kinds of matter. Therefore, each of its constituent parts—Sattwa, Rajas and Tamas—is just as subtle as Prakriti. These three Gunas, Sattwa-Guna, Rajo-Guna, and Tamo-Guna, are so subtle and fine that, compared to them, even photons or sub-atomic particles like electrons and neutrinos are relatively gross. Gunas are finer and subtler than anything that we know of in this world. And yet, according to Sânkhya philosophy, everything in this world, whether gross or subtle, is composed of the three Gunas. The Gunas cannot be directly perceived by us because of their extreme subtlety. Just as we cannot see electricity and yet we know its presence by seeing its manifestation in the form of electric lights, the stove, TV, etc., so also we can indirectly know the presence of the Gunas by seeing their various manifestations. Each Guna has its own distinctive and unique qualities or characteristics. These characteristics manifest themselves through everything in the world. By seeing these characteristics, the presence of the Gunas in things can be inferred.

Sattwa-Guna is light or buoyant, bright or illuminating. It is of the nature of joy. It has the ability to reveal or make

---

1. See page 54.

things known. The luminosity of light, the ability of the mind and senses to know things, the reflecting power of a mirror, and the transparency of glass and crystals are all due to the presence of Sattwa-Guna in them. Similarly, if we see happiness, contentment, satisfaction, joy or bliss in a mind, we should know that it is due to the presence of Sattwa. In the same manner, the lightness or buoyancy of cork or similar substances can be explained in terms of the presence of Sattwa-Guna.

Rajo-Guna[2] causes activity, movement and restlessness. Avarice, hankering, anger, egoism, vanity and the wish to dominate over others are also characteristics of Rajo-Guna. It also is of the nature of pain and suffering—the cause of all types of painful experiences. Wherever we see activity, movement or restlessness, pain or suffering in this world, we should know that it is due to Rajo-Guna.

The characteristics of Tamo-Guna are inertia, passivity, sluggishness, heaviness and negativity. It resists activity or movement. It renders the mind sluggish and incapable of knowing things clearly. It causes confusion, mental depression, bewilderment and ignorance. It induces drowsiness and sleep.

The Gunas share two common characteristics. They are in perpetual conflict with one another, each one trying to subdue the others in order to become predominant.[3] At the same time they cooperate with one another. A candle flame exists through the cooperation of the wick, wax and

---

2. Following the rules of Sanskrit grammar, the words *Rajas* and *Guna* when compounded into a single word become Rajo-Guna. Similarly, the words *Tamas* and *Guna* become Tamo-Guna.
3. *Bhagavad Gîtâ*, 14/10.

fire. The flame will cease to exist without such cooperation. Similarly, the world exists owing to the cooperation
of the three Gunas.

Before creation the Gunas remain in a state of perfect
equilibrium, none claiming preponderance. The process
of creation starts when Prakriti borrows consciousness
from Purusha and begins acting like a conscious entity. At
this point the equilibrium of the Gunas is lost and the
conflict between them starts. As a result of this conflict,
Prakriti starts evolving and changing. The first sign of
Prakriti's conscious activity is seen in its tendency to
change itself. It undergoes a process of gradual transformation, and the final outcome is this manifold universe.
In other words, primordial matter—Prakriti—becomes the
universe through a process of evolution.

As mentioned earlier, according to Sânkhya there are as
many Purushas as there are conscious beings. So far as
conscious individuals are concerned, they are a combination of matter and consciousness. That is to say, they are a
combination of Prakriti and Purusha. But this combination is quite unlike any other combination. It is like a mirror reflecting the moon. The moon appears to have
combined with the mirror and become one with it. Yet, we
know that it has not really combined and become one.
Similar is the relationship between Purusha and Prakriti.

In this context it will be helpful to understand the
Hindu concept of mind. What we commonly call the
mind—the medium with the help of which we know
things—is called in Hindu psychology the Antahkarana.
The Sanskrit word *Antahkarana* literally means the inner
instrument for acquiring knowledge. Roughly speaking,

the word *psyche* is a better counterpart for the word *Antah-karana*. The Antahkarana is given different names, however, depending on its functions.

Let us suppose someone has become aware of an object at a distance, but is unable to see it clearly because it is surrounded by mist. The viewer's Antahkarana cognizes the object but is unable to determine what the object really is. "Is it the stump of a tree, a bear, or a squatting human being?" the viewer wonders. When the Antahkarana has this kind of vacillating cognition, it is given the name Manas. As there is no exact equivalent to the word *Manas* in English, it is inadequately translated as *mind*.

The Antahkarana is given the name Buddhi when it uses the faculty of reasoning (determinative faculty) to decisively determine the true character of the cognized object, and thus acquires the non-vacillating knowledge that the object is neither a man nor a bear, but is definitely the stump of a tree. In the absence of an exact English counterpart of the Sanskrit word *Buddhi*, it is inadequately translated as *intellect*. The Antahkarana is given the name Chitta when it functions as memory.

When someone's Antahkarana makes him or her aware of being an individual different from everything and everyone else, then the Antahkarana is called the ego or Ahankâra. This ego is a factor of separation. It separates a person from every other person or thing.

The first product of the evolution of Prakriti is Mahat or Cosmic Intellect. Ahankâra or Cosmic Ego is the second product of Prakriti. This Cosmic Intellect should not be confused with Cosmic Consciousness. In its true state, Prakriti is unconscious primordial matter. Therefore, none of its evolved products, such as Cosmic Intellect, can be consciousness. Purusha alone is consciousness. Prakriti, though conscious during its evolving stage, can never be consciousness itself. The consciousness of Prakriti is borrowed from Purusha. So also with other evolved products of Prakriti.

In the beginning of creation there were no individual beings. They had not yet been created. Prakriti alone existed in the proximity of Purusha. At the beginning of creation Prakriti was all-pervading and occupied the entire cosmos. Prakriti's existence being cosmic existence, its first evolved state—Mahat (Buddhi) or Intellect—was also cosmic. So also was Prakriti's next evolved state, Cosmic Ego or Ahankâra.

Mahat arose out of the preponderance of the element of Sattwa in Prakriti. It is the natural function of Mahat or Buddhi to manifest itself and other things.

Ahankâra was the second product of Prakriti, and it arose directly out of Mahat. There are three kinds of Cosmic Ego or Ahankâra:

- Ego with a preponderance of Sattwa
- Ego with a preponderance of Rajas
- Ego with a preponderance of Tamas

The egos that are predominantly Sattwic or Tamasic cannot evolve or transform themselves. This energy is supplied by the ego with a preponderance of Rajas—the activity producing Guna. Borrowing energy from this Rajasic ego, the others undergo evolution.

From the ego dominated by Sattwa-Guna evolved the five Sense Organs (Jnânendriya), the five Motor Organs (Karmendriya) and the Mind (Manas). From Tamo-Guna-dominated ego evolved the five subtle physical essences or Tanmâtras. Tanmâtras are so small and so subtle that they cannot be perceived. Their existence can only be known through inference. The word *Tanmâtra* literally means *only that*. The five Tanmâtras are the potential elements or generic essences of sound, touch, color, taste and smell.

From the Tanmâtras evolved the five gross physical elements or Mahâ-bhûtas:

- Space element (Âkâsha)
- Air element (Vâyu)
- Fire element (Agni)
- Water element (Ap)
- Earth element (Kshiti)

These gross physical elements mingled in different proportions following the rules of permutation and combination and became this tangible manifold universe.[4]

One may ask how something as subtle and intangible as the Tanmâtras can become this gross and tangible universe. The answer is given using the analogy of the tiny seed of a gigantic banyan tree. If we dissect the seed, we see no tree in it. Yet in a subtle form the future banyan tree already exists in it. The subtle presence of the tree in the seed will eventually manifest itself as a huge banyan tree. The same is also true of the Tanmâtras.

---

4. For a more detailed account of the evolution of the world, please see *An Introduction To Indian Philosophy* by S. Chatterjee, Ph.D. & D. Datta, Ph.D.; Publishers: University Of Calcutta. 7th Edition. 1968. pp. 267-274.

XV

SAMÂDHI
The Eighth Step

There are two kinds of Samâdhi. One is called Samprajnâta Samâdhi, and the other Asamprajnâta Samâdhi.

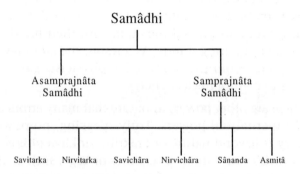

Samprajnâta Samâdhi

Samprajnâta Samâdhi is of six kinds: Savitarka, Nirvitarka, Savichâra, Nirvichâra, Sânanda, and Asmitâ. A Yogî who masters all six kinds of Samprajnâta Samâdhi gains the power to control Nature.

1. Savitarka Samâdhi

The Sanskrit word *Savitarka* means with question, and the expression *Savitarka Samâdhi* means Samâdhi with question. As stated in the preceding chapter, according to

137

Sânkhya philosophy the entire cosmos is composed of five external gross elements called Mahâ-bhûtas. When the mind is concentrated inquiringly on these Mahâ-bhûtas— as though questioning them—the mind attains a Samâdhi called Savitarka Samâdhi. From this Samâdhi is acquired complete knowledge of the gross elements. And along with that knowledge comes the power to control them. Swâmî Vivekânanda says, "Knowledge is power, and as soon as we begin to know a thing we get power over it; so also, when the mind begins to meditate on the different elements it gains power over them."

For instance, the existence of extremely subtle sub-atomic particles was unknown to people for thousands of years. Physicists probed the atom with their highly concentrated inquiring minds. As a result, the atom revealed its secrets. From this knowledge physicists gained the power to control nuclear energy.

There are other powers in nature that many erroneously call supernatural powers. Truly speaking, no power or energy is beyond nature or Prakriti. Sânkhya philosophy, on which these various disciplines of Yoga, such as meditation, are based, sees no difference between energy, matter and the mind. According to this philosophical system, they all are evolved forms of the same Mother Nature or Prakriti. And Prakriti or Mother Nature is no other than the finest primordial matter.

Humans have explored the most inaccessible areas on earth, including even the far-flung polar regions. Nevertheless, there is one area that has yet to be thoroughly explored. That is the area of the human mind. Scientists have yet to know all of its secrets and powers. Most mental powers are still a mystery to scientists, but they are not a mystery to perfected Yogîs. They have come to know all the secrets of their own minds and thus gained power and control over them. How Yogîs by a mere wish or thought perform miracles may well be a mystery to others, but it is not a mystery to them. The powers others call miraculous, supernatural or occult, are all under the control of perfected Yogîs. These powers come naturally to Yogîs with total control over their minds. Yet they may not use their powers unless inspired by God. Unlike scientists who have contributed to the use of nuclear power for destructive purposes, Yogîs never use their powers to harm anybody. Through the practice of Yama and Niyama[1] their minds have become deeply entrenched in the highest moral and ethical principles. It is impossible for them to deviate from these principles.

For advanced students of Râja Yoga, who have not yet reached the goal, some of these powers may come as milestones of spiritual progress. But getting attached to them will be detrimental to the achievement of their spiritual goal. Shrî Krishna and Buddha instructed their disciples never to indulge in these powers.

2. Nirvitarka Samâdhi

When students succeed in concentrating their minds on the gross elements (five Mahâ-bhûtas) by taking them out of time and space and have come to know the gross elements as they truly are, then their minds are said to be in Nirvitarka Samâdhi. The word *Nirvitarka* means without question.

---

1. See Chapters IV and V to know more about Yama and Niyama.

Every object we know is related to time and space. How is it possible to think of an object without relating it to time and space? Is it ever possible to separate an object from time and space? That it can be done may indirectly be explained by the following analogy:

There is an exquisite statue made of pure gold on display in a museum. When we see this statue we are aware of two things: firstly, the form of the statue; and secondly, the gold with which the statue is made. It is not easy to think only of the form of the statue without thinking of the gold. Nor is it ordinarily possible for us to think only of the gold without being aware of the external form of the golden statue.

In special situations these two can be separated. Suppose a world famous art critic has come to the museum. The critic looks at the statue in wonder and admires the external form of the sculpture. The whole mind of the critic is concentrated on the form of the statue, not on the gold. In other words, the critic is only aware of the space occupied by the form of the statue, not the essence that is gold.

Then at midnight when the museum is closed, a burglar eludes the security guards and manages to enter the museum. He looks at the sculpture. All he sees is the gold. He hardly notices the external form of the sculpture. "There must be at least 300 pounds of gold there!" the burglar mutters to himself. His mind is concentrated only on the gold, not on the external form of the statue. He is not aware of the space occupied by the form of the statue—he is only aware of its essence.

Similarly, when meditators with great mastery over concentration can think of an object without relating it to time and space, their minds achieve Nirvitarka Samâdhi.

It is necessary to remember here that Prakriti is the subtlest form of matter. It has gradually evolved step by step into grosser and grosser forms and eventually has become this gross and tangible universe. One may wonder how something as subtle as Prakriti can become transformed into this gross and tangible universe. Water vapor is both invisible and subtle, yet it becomes transformed into tangible water and solid ice. Prof. Albert Einstein—undoubtedly the greatest scientist of this age—also thought that energy and matter are inter-convertible.[2] In other words, something as subtle as energy can become gross matter. This has been known to the Sânkhya philosophers for thousands of years.

If we retrace the path of the evolutionary process by which Prakriti has become this universe, we notice that this tangible universe, composed of five gross elements or Mahâbhûtas, is the grossest form of Prakriti. Then in order of diminishing grossness come the Tanmâtras, the senses, the mind, the Cosmic Ego, the Cosmic Intellect, and last of all Prakriti in her primordial state.

---

2. Einstein's equation $E=mc^2$ inspired later physicists to develop atomic energy by partial conversion of matter. More direct conversion of mass into energy and the converse process are observed in the production of the electron-positron pair through the annihilation of the photon (in the presence of an atom or a nucleus) or in the production of the photon through the annihilation of the electron-positron pair. The relativistic theory of such phenomena is discussed in the book entitled *The Theory of Photons and Electrons* by J.M. Jauch and F. Rohrlich (Addison-Wesley Publ., 1955), 373-379.

In the beginning meditators are unable to concentrate on something as subtle as Prakriti. First they have to learn to concentrate on grosser objects and then gradually learn to concentrate on subtler ones. For this reason meditators have to first concentrate on the gross elements or Mahâbhûtas. When they succeed in that kind of concentration, they achieve Savitarka Samâdhi. Then comes the next higher step of concentration, Nirvitarka Samâdhi. In this manner, in order of increasing subtlety they have to concentrate step by step on the Tanmâtras, the mind and the ego. When they gain perfect concentration at these levels they gradually achieve Savichâra, Nirvichâra, Sânanda and Asmitâ Samâdhis. (They don't have to concentrate on the senses.)

3. Savichâra Samâdhi

The word *Savichâra* means with discrimination. When meditators go one step higher than Nirvitarka Samâdhi and concentrate on the Tanmâtras by thinking of them existing in time and space, they attain Savichâra Samâdhi.

4. Nirvichâra Samâdhi

In the next higher level meditators concentrate on the Tanmâtras by eliminating the awareness of time and space. Then they attain a higher Samâdhi called Nirvichâra Samâdhi. The word *Nirvichâra* literally means without discrimination.

5. Sânanda Samâdhi

This Samâdhi, also called the blissful Samâdhi, is superior to Nirvichâra Samâdhi. The reader must have noticed by now that the meditators are gradually becoming able to concentrate on finer and finer objects and are thus able to have higher and higher levels of Samâdhi. When they concentrate on the mind itself using it as the object of their meditation, and think of the mind as bereft of the qualities of activity (Rajas) and dullness (Tamas), then they achieve Sânanda Samâdhi.

6. Asmitâ Samâdhi

In this highest state of Samprajnâta Samâdhi the mind is only aware of its ego or Asmitâ after separating it from Rajas and Tamas. In this Samâdhi only the awareness of the Sattwa state of the ego remains. In this state meditators are able to think of themselves as devoid of the gross body. The scriptures call such persons Videhî—those who have lost consciousness of their gross bodies. Yet the sense of their individuality has not been lost. They are still in the domain of Prakriti or Mother Nature, and are, in fact, now merged in Prakriti. This state is called the Prakritilaya state in Sanskrit. It is an extremely exalted state. Now they have all the powers needed to control nature. Nevertheless, they have not yet arrived at the goal of spiritual life. They have yet to attain total freedom from matter or Prakriti. They are yet to know that they are not a product of Prakriti, but are the eternal Divine Spirit. Total freedom will be attained only when their little individualities are lost and they regain their Divine Identity. For those persons there is still another higher step to climb—another Samâdhi to be attained. That Samâdhi is Asamprajnâta Samâdhi.

Asamprajnâta Samâdhi

This Samâdhi is the acme of concentration. It is attained by constantly practicing the cessation of all activities of the mind, or Chitta. In his Yoga system Patanjali uses the

word *Chitta* to mean the mind. In Asamprajnâta Samâdhi
the Chitta retains only the unmanifested impressions, and
nothing else. The great Swâmî Vivekânanda, who himself
had this Samâdhi, has described the nature of Asamprajnâta Samâdhi as follows:

> This is the perfect super-conscious,[3] Asamprajnâta
> Samâdhi, the state that gives us freedom. The first
> state (i.e. any of the varieties of Samprajnâta
> Samâdhi) does not give us freedom, does not liber-
> ate the soul. A man may attain to all powers, and
> yet fall again. There is no safeguard until the soul
> goes beyond nature (i.e. Prakriti). It is very diffi-
> cult to do so although the method seems easy. The
> method is to meditate on the mind itself, and
> whenever thought comes, to strike it down, allow-
> ing no thought to come into the mind, thus mak-
> ing it an entire vacuum. When we can really do
> this, that very moment we shall attain liberation.
> When persons without training and preparation
> try to make their minds vacant they are likely to
> succeed only in covering themselves with Tamas,
> the material of ignorance, which makes the mind
> dull and stupid, and leads them to think that they
> are making a vacuum of the mind. To be able to
> really do that is to manifest the greatest strength,
> the highest control.
>
> When this state Asamprajnâta—super-conscious-
> ness—is reached, the Samâdhi becomes seedless.
> What is meant by that? In a concentration where
> there is no consciousness, where the mind suc-
> ceeds only in quelling the waves of the Chitta and

---

3. To understand the meaning of the term *super-conscious* in re-
lation to Asamprajnâta Samâdhi, please see page 8.

holding them down, the waves remain in the form of tendencies. These tendencies (or seeds) become waves again, when the time comes. But when you have destroyed all these tendencies, almost destroyed the mind, then the Samâdhi becomes seedless; there are no more seeds in the mind out of which to manufacture again and again this plant of life, this ceaseless round of birth and death.

You may ask, what state would that be, in which there is no mind, there is no knowledge? What we call knowledge is a lower state than the one beyond knowledge. You must always bear in mind that the extremes look very much alike. If a very low vibration of ether is taken as darkness, an intermediate state as light, very high vibration will be darkness again. Similarly, ignorance is the lowest state, knowledge is the middle state, and beyond knowledge is the highest state, the two extremes of which seem to be the same. Knowledge itself is a manufactured something, a combination; it is not Reality.

What is the result of constant practice of this higher concentration? All old tendencies of restlessness (Rajas), and dullness (Tamas), will be destroyed, as well as the tendencies of goodness (Sattwa) too. The case is similar to that of the chemicals used to take the dirt and alloy off gold. When the ore is melted down, the dross is burnt along with the chemicals. So this constant controlling power will stop the previous bad tendencies, and, eventually, the good ones also. Those good and evil tendencies will suppress each other leaving alone the soul, in its own splendor,

untrammeled by either good or bad, the omni-
present, omnipotent, and omniscient. Then the
man will know he neither had birth nor death,
nor need of heaven or earth. He will know that he
neither came nor went, it was nature which was
moving, and that movement was reflected upon
the soul. The form of the light reflected by the
glass upon the wall moves, and the wall foolishly
thinks it is moving. So with all of us; it is the
Chitta (Mind) constantly moving, making itself
into various forms, and we think that we are these
various forms. All these delusions will vanish.
When that free Soul will command—not pray or
beg, but command—then whatever It desires will
be immediately fulfilled; whatever It wants It will
be able to do.[4]

It has been mentioned that Asamprajnâta Samâdhi is
Samâdhi par excellence, it is the acme of concentration.
This Samâdhi, according to the nondualistic school of
Vedânta philosophy, is called Nirvikalpa Samâdhi. Some
also call it Sthita Samâdhi or Jada Samâdhi. The following
comparison will give a good idea of what Asamprajnâta
Samâdhi is: When meditators can concentrate their minds
on the object of their meditation for 12 seconds, it is
called Dhâranâ. When the period of concentration is 12
times that of Dhâranâ (i.e. 144 seconds), it is called
Dhyâna. When the concentration lasts for twelve times
the period of Dhyâna, it is called Asamprajnâta Samâdhi.
In other words, when meditators can concentrate their
minds without any break for 28 minutes and 48 seconds,
they attain Asamprajnâta Samâdhi. To accomplish this

4. Swâmî Vivekânanda, *Râja Yoga* (New York: Râmakrishna-
Vivekânanda Center, 1982), 115-118.

takes many years of steady and relentless practice under the guidance of proper teachers. There is no shortcut to Samâdhi.

Shrî Râmakrishna describes Sthita Samâdhi/Jada Samâdhi/Nirvikalpa Samâdhi as follows, "In Sthita Samâdhi the aspirant totally loses outer consciousness and remains in that state a long time, maybe for many days."

The scriptures of Bhakti (the path of devotion) talk about Chetana Samâdhi. This Samâdhi is attained by devotees because of their intense love of God. "In this Samâdhi there remains the consciousness of 'I'—the 'I' of the servant-and-Master relationship, of the lover-and-beloved relationship, and of the enjoyer-and-Food relationship. God is the Master; the devotee is the servant. God is the beloved; the devotee is the lover. God is the Food, and the devotee is the enjoyer."[5] Chetana Samâdhi is also called Bhâva Samâdhi.

Shrî Râmakrishna mentions another kind of Samâdhi called Unmanâ Samâdhi. He says, "When the aspirant withdraws his mind suddenly from all sense objects and unites it with God it is called Unmanâ Samâdhi."

---

5. *The Gospel of Sri Ramakrishna* (New York: Ramakrishna-Vivekananda Center, 1942), 478.

XVI

WHAT HAPPENS AFTER SAMÂDHI?

What happens to the mind when it goes into Samâdhi? According to the Yoga scriptures, the mind becomes one with Brahman (Divinity) during Samâdhi, just as salt when dissolved becomes one with water. In that state the mind has only Brahman-consciousness, it does not have consciousness of this world.

Is it possible to bring the mind that has become dissolved in the ocean of Brahman back to the awareness of this world? The answer is both "Yes" and "No." Some Yogîs can bring their minds back to the awareness of this world, while others cannot.

Different spiritual levels according to various Yoga sources

Some treatises on Yoga[1] mention seven levels of spiritual progress that can be attained step by step. They are as follows:

1. Shubhech-chhâ
2. Vichâ-ranâ
3. Tanu-mânasâ
4. Sattâ-patti

---

1. *E.g. Vâshishtha Râmâyana.* Utpattiprakarana—Sarga 118.

The seven levels of spiritual progress according to Yoga Philosophy

Yoga Level	Name of the Yoga Level	Category of Spiritual Aspirants	Their Experiences	Characteristics
First	Shubhech-chhā	Sādhaka (spiritual aspirant)	They are aware of the external world and unaware of Brahman.	They consider multiplicity as real.
Second	Vichā-ranā	Sādhaka (spiritual aspirant)	Even though they have made some spiritual progress they are still unaware of Brahman.	They consider multiplicity as real.
Third	Tanu-mānasā	Sādhaka (spiritual aspirant)	Although they are more advanced than those of the first two levels, they are still unaware of Brahman.	They consider multiplicity as real.
Fourth	Sattā-patti	Brahma-vit (Siddha or knower of Brahman)	They are aware of the world but to them the world appears to be a dream, not real. Brahman alone is real.	They consider multiplicity as unreal and Brahman alone as real.
Fifth	Asang-sakti	Brahma-vid-vara (Siddha Jivanmukta)	They are as though in a dreamless sleep. Even the "world-dream" is no longer there. They have only Brahman-consciousness. It is a Samādhi state.	They can return to the awareness of the world by themselves.
Sixth	Padārtha-bhāvini	Brahma-vid-varīān (Siddha Jivanmukta)	They are as though in a deeper dreamless sleep. No awareness of the world—a state of deeper Samādhi. They have only Brahman-consciousness.	They can be made to return to the awareness of the world only through the efforts of others.
Seventh	Turyagā	Brahma-vid-varishtha (Siddha Jivanmukta)	They are as though in the deepest dreamless sleep. No awareness at all of the world—a state of deepest Samādhi. In this state they have only Brahman-consciousness.	They cannot return to the awareness of the world. Only divine incarnations can come back from this highest state of Samādhi.

5. Asang-sakti
6. Padârthâ-bhâvinî
7. Turyagâ

Shubhech-chhâ is the lowermost level of spiritual growth. In ascending order, the second and the third levels are Vichâ-ranâ and Tanu-mânasâ respectively. Spiritual aspirants belonging to these three levels are called Sâdhakas. Sâdhakas (spiritual aspirants) are conscious of this world and have not gone beyond the awareness of the multiplicity or plurality existing here.

The fourth level is Sattâ-patti. A person at this level is called a Siddha or a Brahma-vit (a knower of Brahman). To Siddhas or Brahma-vits the world appears to be a dream. They gain the experiential conviction that Brahman alone is real. They experience Brahman pervading in and through everything as the Divine Essence, and to them the world is but an appearance on Brahman. To them Brahman is like a movie screen and the world is like a movie projected on it.

Those who belong to the fifth level, Asang-sakti, have had the experience of Samâdhi. Such a person is superior to a Brahma-vit, and is called a Brahma-vid-vara.

The sixth level is Padârthâ-bhâvinî. Those belonging to this level have had deeper Samâdhi than that of Brahma-vid-varas, and someone attaining this level is called a Brahma-vid-varîân.

The seventh and the highest level is Turyagâ. Those belonging to this level are superior to Brahma-vid-varîâns. They have experienced the deepest Samâdhi. One who has experienced this Samâdhi is called a Brahma-vid-varish-tha.

Brahma-vid-varas, Brahma-vid-variâns and Brahma-vid-varishthas are called Siddha Jîvan-muktas or living liberated souls. All have had the experience of Samâdhi. The fifth, sixth and seventh levels—Asang-sakti, Padârthâ-bhâvinî and Turyagâ—are three different stages of Samâdhi, each successive one deeper than the preceding.

While in Samâdhi these living liberated souls (Siddha Jîvanmuktas) have only Brahman-consciousness. They no longer are aware of this world. To the world they appear to be in a deep sleep, yet they are fully awake in the domain of Brahman-consciousness. In that state they do not have any body-consciousness. Just as people wake up on their own from sleep, so also Brahma-vid-varas, by their own efforts, can awaken themselves from Samâdhi. Such awakening in Sanskrit is called Vy-utthâna.

But the Brahma-vid-variâns' Samâdhi is much deeper. They cannot rouse themselves from the Padârthâ-bhâvinî level of Samâdhi. They have to be awakened by others. Such awakening is done by chanting the holy name of God very loudly into the ears of the person in Samâdhi.

An example of this kind of awakening has been described in an article in the 19th century Bengali periodical *Dharma-tattwa*, published by the Brâhmo Samâj[2] of India. The article is dated September 16, 1886. It describes Shrî Râmakrishna's first meeting with the famous Brâhmo leader Keshab Chandra Sen of Calcutta. The relevant por-

---

2. Brâhmo Samâj, or the Society of Brâhmos, was a reformist Hindu church founded in the 19th century by Râmmohan Roy. Keshab Chandra Sen, a successor of Râmmohan Roy, turned out to be the most renowned Brâhmo leader of his time. He was a great orator and scholar.

tion of the article, as translated by the author, is given below:

> He (Shrî Râmakrishna) entered into Samâdhi while singing a devotional song. By seeing his Samâdhi the (Brâhmo) preachers present there did not think of it as a high spiritual experience. They concluded that it was some kind of trick. But as soon as Shrî Râmakrishna had entered into Samâdhi, Hriday Bhattâchârya (Shrî Râmakrishna's nephew who had accompanied him) started chanting (the Holy Word) "Om" very loudly and requested others also to join. After a little while the Paramahamsa (i.e., Shrî Râmakrishna) partially recovered consciousness and started smiling. Then with great spiritual fervor he started talking about many deep and profound spiritual truths. At this, the (Brâhmo) preachers were astounded. They realized that Râmakrishna was a Divine Person; he was not an ordinary man.

The Brahma-vid-varishthas' Samâdhi is at the Turyagâ level. It is so deep that no one can awaken them. Sometimes their hearts stop beating and they appear to be dead. Having lost body-consciousness they cannot eat or drink. They can no longer be roused from this Samâdhi. Deprived of nutrition, their bodies die in a matter of days, dropping off like dry leaves.

Nobody needs to grieve over the death of Brahma-vid-varishthas. Having experienced their spiritual identity with Brahman through Samâdhi, they become free from body-consciousness. They also gain the experience that as Eternal Spirit, they are birthless and deathless. The deaths of their bodies are of no consequence to them.

Shrî Chaitanya Mahâprabhu
(1485-1533)

Only Divine Incarnations can awake from Turyagâ Samâdhi

Divine Incarnations,[3] however, can return even from the Turyagâ state of Samâdhi whenever they wish. They are exceptions to the rule.[4] Shrî Chaitanya Mahâprabhu (1485—1533) was one of the most exalted spiritual personalities of India. Thousands look upon him as a Divine Incarnation. He used to have Bhâva Samâdhi frequently. He also often entered into other kinds of Samâdhi, including Turyagâ Samâdhi, and came out of them easily. Once on the seashore off the coast of Purî[5] he entered into Turyagâ Samâdhi. Losing body-consciousness he fell into the sea. Many hours later fishermen retrieved his body with their net. Although he had no outer signs of life due to Turyagâ Samâdhi, he gradually recovered full consciousness to the joy and happiness of his disciples.

Recent examples of genuine saints and godmen who have had Samâdhi

During the past two centuries India has had some great saints of proven reliability. Their reputation for saintliness has stood the test of time and in their exalted lives we see the various characteristics of Samâdhi.

---

3. The idea of a Divine Incarnation, also called an Avatâra in Sanskrit, is found mainly in the Hindu Smriti scriptures like the *Bhagavad Gîtâ* and *Shrîmad Bhâgavatam*. The Vedas do not clearly speak of Avatâras. The counterpart of the expression *Avatâra* in Sânkhya philosophy is Îshwarakoti. Îshwarakotis can wake up from the Turyagâ level of Samâdhi.
4. See *The Gospel of Sri Ramakrishna* translated by Swâmî Nikhilânanda (New York: Ramakrishna-Vivekananda Center, 1942), 237.
5. A famous place of pilgrimage in India.

Shrî Trailanga Swâmî
(c1737-1887)

Shrî Trailanga Swâmî (c1737–1887)

Shrî Trailanga Swâmî was a famous Yogî and saint of Banaras. His life spanned the major parts of both the 18th and 19th centuries. For nearly 150 years Trailanga Swâmî lived in the holy city of Banaras, which is called Vârânasî today. In the later part of his life the Swâmî remained immersed in Samâdhi most of the time. He was a Brahma-vid-varishtha. At the age of 150 he gave up his body in Samâdhi. Shrî Râmakrishna, who had met this great Swâmî, said that he had no sense of individuality left in him. He had become totally identified with Shiva (God).

Shrî Râmakrishna (1836-1886)

Shrî Râmakrishna frequently entered into various kinds of Samâdhi. One of them was Chetana Samâdhi or Bhâva Samâdhi. This Samâdhi is usually associated with specific spiritual moods and has often been mentioned in the Vaishnava scriptures. In this Samâdhi Shrî Râmakrishna communed with God and yet retained partial consciousness of this world.

On one occasion when Shrî Râmakrishna had Bhâva Samâdhi during a visit to his ancestral home in his native village, Kamarpukur, his soul started swimming blissfully like a fish in the ocean of Brahman-consciousness. Some of his women relatives were present around him and talking loudly. One of them said, "Girls, don't talk so loudly. Gadâi (Shrî Râmakrishna's nickname) is now swimming like a fish in the ocean of Brahman. You mustn't disturb him!" Shrî Râmakrishna, who had not lost his outer consciousness completely, heard those words. When his Samâdhi was over he wondered how that lady had come to know what he had experienced in Bhâva Samâdhi. She must have been a highly advanced soul. How else could she have known?[6]

Shrî Râmakrishna also frequently entered the Asang-sakti level of Samâdhi and would wake up on his own. When in the Padârthâ-bhâvinî level of Samâdhi, others had to awaken him.[7]

Like Shrî Chaitanya Mahâprabhu he would often enter the Turyagâ level of Samâdhi and return from it. Judging by this and other characteristics detailed in the Vaishnava scriptures, several famous pundits of Bengal declared him to be a Divine Incarnation. Pundit Padmalochan, Pundit Vaishnavacharan Goswâmî and Pundit Gaurîkânta Bhattâchârya Tarkabhûshan were among them.[8]

While living in the temple of the Divine Mother Kâlî in Dakshineswar, he often entered Nirvikalpa or Asampra-jnâta Samâdhi. Once, losing body-consciousness, he remained in that Samâdhi for six months. Although he was completely unaware of the outer world, the vital functions of his body still continued. As though sent by God, a wandering monk happened to come to that temple and remained there those six months. He kept Shrî Râmakrishna alive by forcing food and water down him until he awoke from his Samâdhi. Sometimes, during these deep Samâdhis Shrî Râmakrishna's heart would stop beating and his body would became stiff, displaying signs

---

6. Unfortunately we do not know that lady's name. She may have been one of Shrî Râmakrishna's close relatives, perhaps an elder sister.
7. See page 152.
8. See *Srî Râmakrishna—The Great Master* by Swâmî Sâradânan-da—translated into English by Swâmî Jagadânanda (Mylapore, Madras: Srî Râmakrishna Math, 1952), 305.

of death. Defying medical science, however, after a while he would regain consciousness and resume his normal activities.

On another occasion, while talking to the devotees, Shrî Râmakrishna suddenly entered into a very deep Samâdhi. While in Samâdhi his heart stopped beating and he had no outer signs of life. A medical doctor touched Shrî Râmakrishna's eyeball with his fingertip to check his corneal reflexes. In those days, doctors confirmed the death of a patient by this test. Medical science then was not aware of the electrical activity of the brain. Therefore, the question of using an electroencephalograph could not arise. The doctor detected no corneal reflex and concluded that Shrî Râmakrishna had died. Yet, after a short while he awoke from his Samâdhi and started talking normally. This astounded the doctor.

Shrî Ramana Maharshi (1880-1949)

This renowned saint of Tiruvannâmalai in South India is another exemplar. When he was sixteen years old he had a strange experience while living in his uncle's house. He was alone in an upstairs room when a terrible fear of death suddenly overwhelmed him. Then, at his own choosing, he went through a simulated experience of death and suddenly realized that in his real nature he was birthless and deathless. His real nature was not related to the body, mind or personality.

This experience totally transformed him. From then onward he could no longer think of himself as an individual. His little individuality had melted away in that Imperishable Consciousness, Brahman, which is beyond all limitations. Six weeks later he renounced the world and

Shrî Ramana Maharshi
(1880-1949)
(Photograph courtesy of the
Society of Abidance in Truth)

went to Tiruvannâmalai, a holy city in South India, many miles away from his hometown. He took shelter at the temple of Lord Arunâchaleswara in Tiruvannâmalai. There, occasionally he would become deeply immersed in Divine Consciousness. While in that state he had no body-consciousness nor consciousness of the world. There were festering insect bites all over his legs yet he was not aware of them. He was rarely conscious enough to eat or drink, and his body became extremely emaciated. During that period his hair and fingernails grew to unmanageable lengths.[9]

Is this condition Samâdhi? Judging by the signs and symptoms, it certainly appears to be so. But what kind of Samâdhi? His biographers call it Sahaja Samâdhi. According to the Yoga scriptures, he seems to have been in the Asang-sakti level of Samâdhi. He roused himself from that state off and on. Therefore, we can be sure that he was at least a Brahma-vid-vara or Siddha Jîvan-mukta, and perhaps something higher.

How a Yogî's mind, dissolved in Brahman, can be brought back to the awareness of the world

As mentioned earlier, just as salt gets dissolved in water and becomes one with it, a Yogî's mind, when in Samâdhi, becomes dissolved in the infinite ocean of Divine Consciousness. At that time the Yogî is no longer conscious of his body or this world.

---

9. Sources: David Godman, *The Teachings of Sri Ramana Maharshi* (Penguin Books, 1985) and Arthur Osborne, *Ramana Maharshi and the Path of Self Knowledge* (London: Rider And Company, 1954).

Since the Yogî's mind in Samâdhi becomes dissolved in Divine Consciousness or Brahman, one may wonder how the Yogî can bring it back to the awareness of this world. The scriptures of Hinduism explain this using a technical Sanskrit term—*Lesha-Avidyâ*. Some souls who are extremely compassionate towards mankind can retain a trace of their compassionate thought even in Samâdhi. This thought is called Lesha-Avidyâ. It is Lesha-Avidyâ that drags their minds back to the awareness of this world. Retaining this trace of compassion is possible due to the Prârabdha Karma[10] of the Yogîs.

A little knowledge of chemistry can help explain how Lesha Avidyâ can bring down the minds of Yogîs from Samâdhi: If one goes on adding salt to a glass of water and continually stirs it with a spoon, the salt starts dissolving and forms a saline solution. As more and more salt is added to the solution it becomes more and more saturated with salt. At last it becomes so saturated that no more salt can be dissolved in it. This highly concentrated solution is

---

10. According to the Doctrine of Karma every action produces an effect, either good or bad. The word *Karma* means action. In this particular context it means the effect of action. Prârabdha Karma means the effect of action which has become available to the doer. Not all actions produce effects that are readily available to the doer. Some actions produce effects which come later. They are like term deposits in banks. The interest accrued on each term deposit becomes available to the depositor only at the time of its maturity. Similarly, some effects of actions may not even be available during the lifetime of the doer. Even if the doer dies, these effects do not get lost. They remain securely stored. They remain accumulated till their time of maturity. At the time of maturity these effects, also called Prârabdha Karma, force the doer to be born again in order to suffer or enjoy according to the nature of his Prârabdha Karma.

called a supersaturated solution. If a single crystal of salt now be put in this supersaturated solution, something strange will start happening. This added crystal will start the process of recrystallization. As a result, some of the dissolved salt will come out of the solution as 100% pure salt crystals.

Lesha-Avidyâ, or the lingering thought of compassion in the minds of Yogîs, works exactly like the crystal that starts the recrystallization process. The thought of compassion for suffering humanity, or Lesha Avidyâ, brings down the Yogîs' minds from Samâdhi to the awareness of this world. Like recrystallized salt, their minds coming out of Samâdhi are also 100% pure. Using these minds, illumined Yogîs interact with the world.

The behavior of a knower of Brahman after Samâdhi

Knowers of Brahman are not conscious of their bodies. The *Shrîmad Bhâgavatam* (11/13/36) says that a knower of Brahman is like a person who is completely drunk. The drunken person is not even aware if he or she has clothes on or if they have dropped off. Similarly, knowers of Brahman are not aware if their bodies are still there, moving around, or have dropped off. Others, however, will see their bodies, even though the knowers of Brahman are totally unaware of the existence of their own bodies. This is the state of a Jîvanmukta—a person liberated here and now.

According to Shrî Râmakrishna, a spiritually unillumined person is like a coconut. A coconut has a thick outer coating of fibers covering its hard oval shell. The shell has a thick, white layer of coconut meat clinging to its inner surface. The rest is filled with water. In this analogy the outer hard shell is the body-mind-complex of the spiritually unillumined person and the nut the soul. In this case the soul is attached to the body-mind-complex.

On the other hand, a Jîvanmukta is like a dry coconut. All the water in it has dried up, making the nut completely dry. Due to loss of moisture the nut has shrunk and become detached from the shell. It has now become reduced to an oval nutty ball with a hollow center. If you shake the coconut you can hear the ball rolling inside the shell. In this analogy the nut—the soul—has become completely free from the shell—the body-mind-complex. Yet, the soul is maintaining a point of contact with it. Simi-

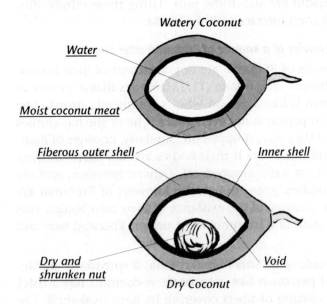

Coconut cross-section

larly, the soul of a Jîvanmukta maintains a point of contact with the body-mind-complex. Because of this point of contact, it is possible for the Jîvanmukta to interact with the outside world, give spiritual teachings or engage in other activities to benefit humankind.

A Jîvanmukta experiences Divinity as the essence of every thing and every being. To such a person the Divine Essence alone is real. It is the Divine Essence that is being manifested through multifarious forms. To him or her the world appears to be like a motion picture. While watching a movie a viewer interacts with whatever happens in the movie, crying when it is sad, or horrified when it is scary. Yet, no matter what the reaction to the movie, the viewer experiences great joy in watching because he or she knows that nothing in the movie is real.

In the same way, a Jîvanmukta reacts to the happenings in the world. The Jîvanmukta may display fluctuations of mood while interacting with others, but still will be experiencing a continuous undercurrent of joy. To a Jîvanmukta nothing that happens in the world is real—Divinity alone is real. In this state any interaction with the world is a most joyous and rewarding experience, because it is no other than directly interacting with Divinity. The Jîvanmukta sees herself or himself as a part of a Divine play where Divinity is playing all the roles, including the role of a Jîvanmukta. There is no more identification with the body-mind-complex that is subject to birth, change, decay, and death. The unshakable conviction is gained that one is the eternal Divine Spirit—deathless and birthless.

XVII

JAPA

A Spiritual Discipline Complementary To Meditation

From the preceding chapters it must have been recognized that it is not easy for most people to master meditation. Even Patanjali, the greatest exponent of Yoga and meditation, was aware of this. As an alternative to Yoga disciplines, he prescribed Îshwara-Pranidhâna or devotion to God. Shrî Râmakrishna supports Patanjali's view, saying that in this stressful age the path of devotion or Bhakti Yoga is the best and easiest spiritual discipline for most people. As a devotional practice, chanting the holy name of God or Japa is considered extremely efficacious.

The benefits of Japa

Japa is a time-honored technique that enables one to gain control over the mind, purify it, master concentration, and eventually have God-vision. This technique consists of chanting a holy name of God or a prayer over and over again. In Hindu tradition such a word or prayer is called a Mantra. According to Patanjali, a spiritual aspirant can realize God by the repetition of a Mantra.[1]

---

1. *Yoga-Sûtras,* 2/44.

Three main techniques of Japa

Japa can be done in three ways:

1. Chanting aloud—Vâchika Japa.
2. Whispering—Upângshu Japa. The chanters
    move their lips and tongues while whispering
    the holy word, but only the chanters can hear
    it.
3. Silent chanting—Mânasa Japa. In this tech-
    nique the holy word is chanted mentally
    without creating any audible sound.

Among these three, silent chanting (Mânasa Japa) is the
most effective. Whispering the holy word (Upângshu
Japa) is second best. And chanting aloud (Vâchika Japa) is
the least efficacious. Yet each is able to help one to gradually control, purify and concentrate the mind and eventually have God-vision.

Why is silent chanting preferable to whispering or
chanting aloud? In the first place, it requires greater concentration and control over the mind to chant silently.
For that reason, beginners initially find it harder to practice. Nevertheless, those practicing silent chanting can
master their minds much faster than those who use the
other two techniques. And secondly, it is good not to display our spiritual practices before others in order to get
praise or appreciation. Hindu as well as Christian traditions encourage us to keep our spiritual lives secret. Jesus
instructed his followers to pray privately "inside the clos-
ets" of their homes, not in public. Thus, as mental Japa is
not obvious to others, it is better than the other two techniques.

Japa should not be performed at either a very fast pace or too slowly. A medium pace is the best. It is most efficacious if the meaning of the Mantra is remembered while it is chanted.

Four other techniques of Japa

Besides the above, the following four other techniques of Japa are also offered by Hinduism.

The first technique is to repeatedly write the holy name of God a certain number of times a day. This is called Likhita Japa.

The second method is to chant the Mantra silently and continuously for a fixed period of time. This is called Akhanda Japa. Sometimes, as in a relay race, different spiritual aspirants present in a temple or a shrine successively do Akhanda Japa without a break. This kind of Akhanda Japa is usually done from sunrise till sunset.

The third way, used by the Gaudiya Vaishnava sect of Hinduism, is to sing the holy name of God rhythmically to the accompaniment of drums and cymbals. This is called Nâma Sankîrtana. Sometimes this is done without a break for a day, a week, or even a month. This kind of continuous Nâma Sankîrtana is called Akhanda Nâma Sankîrtana. Both Nâma Sankîrtana and Akhanda Nâma Sankîrtana can be done either individually or in a group, depending on the duration of such chanting. Nâma Sankîrtana was introduced by Shrî Chaitanya.

The fourth technique, called Ajapâ Japa,[2] is to perform Japa mentally at every breath. Apajâ Japa also refers to a

---

2. Swâmî Swâhânanda, *Meditation And Other Spiritual Disciplines* (Mayavati, India: Advaita Ashrama, 1994), 13.

state which occurs after Mânasa Japa has been practiced regularly for a number of years and the mind automatically starts chanting the Mantra without any persuasion. This form of Ajapâ Japa—automatic chanting of the Mantra—indicates that we have gained a considerable degree of control over our minds.

Bîja-Mantra

A Bîja-Mantra or a Bîja is a monosyllabic holy word. The Sanskrit word *Bîja* literally means a seed. Therefore, a Bîja-Mantra can be called a Seed-Mantra. Most Bîja-Mantras are a contribution of the Tantra tradition of Hinduism. This tradition claims that a Mantra containing a Bîja is much more powerful than others. According to the Tantra tradition, each deity has a specific Bîja-Mantra. For example, Klîng is the Bîja-Mantra of the Divine Mother Kâlî, while Dung is the Bîja-Mantra of the Divine Mother Durgâ. The sages of the Tantra tradition say that wherever a Bîja-Mantra of a deity is chanted with devotion, the deity becomes manifest there. Such is the power of a Bîja-Mantra. Following scriptural rules, Bîja-Mantras can be used as prefixes to different holy names of God.

The Vedas also have a Bîja-Mantra called Pranava. It is the syllable Om. Like the Bîja-Mantras of the Tantra tradition, the Pranava is frequently used as a prefix to different holy names of God. For example, each of the holy names Shiva and Vishnu may be combined with Pranava to form composite Mantras, such as Om Shiva and Om Vishnu.

Siddha-Mantra

According to Hindu tradition, the holy word or Mantra has to be given to the student by a competent teacher. A Mantra that has helped people to have God-vision is called a Siddha-Mantra. It has great spiritual potency. A Mantra picked from a book may help, but a Mantra given by a God-realized soul is energized by the spiritual power of the giver. Chanting such a Mantra hastens God-realization. For this reason, spiritual aspirants in India want to receive Mantras from God-realized souls. Why such a Mantra is so effective can be explained by the following analogy:

A man has just returned from his medical check-up. He is extremely upset because he has been told that he has cancer. His wife tries to comfort him saying, "Don't worry, darling, you'll get cured!"

His young son says, "Daddy, don't worry, you'll be cured!" But their words give him no comfort whatsoever.

A few days later he goes to the best cancer specialist in the country. After examining him thoroughly the specialist says, "Your cancer has been detected at a very early stage; don't worry, you'll be completely cured." The words of the specialist instantly relieve him of all his worry and anxiety.

His wife, son and the specialist—all have said more or less same comforting words to him. Why then have the specialist's words had such a great impact, while the words of his wife and son have not? Because the cancer specialist's many years of experience are behind his words. Similarly, a Mantra given to a disciple by a God-realized soul has the illumined soul's entire life's spiritual experience behind it. Such a Mantra is not like any other word, it has great spiritual potency. It can help one make faster spiritual progress.

Students who have received Siddha-Mantras from a teacher should chant the Mantra regularly for a certain number of times, as instructed by the teacher. They should chant every day at specified times, preferably in the morning and evening, sitting in a comfortable posture with their backbones erect and their heads and necks held vertically in a straight line. Rosaries may be used to keep count of how many times they have chanted the Mantra. Following their teacher's instructions, they should gradually increase the number of times they chant the Mantra. It will be harmful if on their own they increase the number by fits and starts.

In addition to performing Japa at the specified time, the students should also try to do Mânasa Japa (silent chanting) throughout the day and night as many times as possible. They can do it while lying in bed, sitting or moving around. They need not keep count of such chanting.

How Japa helps in gaining control over the mind

One characteristic of an uncontrolled mind is that it gets bored doing the same thing over and over again. Japa is repeatedly chanting the same Mantra. An uncontrolled mind is reluctant to do such monotonous chanting. In spite of this reluctance, the mind should be persuaded again and again to chant the same Mantra. Eventually the mind, unless otherwise occupied, will chant the Mantra on its own without any persuasion. This is a clear indication that the mind has to a considerable extent come under control.

How Japa purifies the mind

A piece of white cloth takes on the color of the dye in which it is soaked. The mind is also like a piece of white cloth. It absorbs the good or bad qualities of its thoughts. God is the holiest of the holy. A Mantra contains the name of God and is, therefore, equally holy. As mentioned earlier, Japa consists of repeatedly chanting a Mantra. A mind performing Japa is thinking of holiness continually, and will gradually become holy and pure.

How Japa helps in mastering concentration

When we perform Japa we have to articulate the Mantra correctly and listen to it intently. We must not allow the mind to drift anywhere else. This practice will eventually enable us to gain great concentration.

To get tangible results Japa has to be performed regularly and intensely for several years. There is no instant success in spiritual life. In order to have genuine spiritual experiences, we have to steadfastly and intensely practice Japa for several years under the guidance of our teachers.

Once a disciple came to his teacher Shrî Sârada Devî (1853-1920), the well-known woman saint of India, and said to her, "I've been chanting my Mantra every day for several years and haven't noticed any tangible spiritual progress yet. What should I do?"

Sârada Devî replied, "My child, if you want to notice tangible results you should chant your Mantra 10,000 times a day." The disciple did as he was instructed and eventually was blessed with genuine spiritual visions. It should be noted here that immediately after getting a Mantra students must not start chanting it many thousand times. As mentioned earlier, they should gradually increase the number of repetitions strictly under their teacher's guidance. Otherwise, it may harm them.

The necessity for patience and steadfastness in the practice of Japa

Many spiritual aspirants become discouraged after doing Japa for a year or two because they notice no tangible spiritual progress. They should realize that spiritual progress takes place steadily but imperceptibly. It is like growing from childhood to adulthood. It takes time. Let us suppose a little boy wants to grow as tall as his father. If he measures his height every five minutes, will he ever notice any growth? Yet he is continuously growing. The same is true of spiritual progress.

In this connection another factor needs to be discussed. Suppose we perform Japa for two hours a day. This must produce some beneficial effect on our minds. But the impact of our secular activities done during the remaining twenty-two hours of the day will surely outweigh the impact of Japa done for only two hours. This is why we may not notice any tangible spiritual progress. In order to see results, we should mentally chant the Mantra as many times as possible throughout the rest of our waking hours under the teacher's guidance.

The technique of spiritualizing secular activities

The other alternative is to spiritualize all secular activities. No matter what work we do, we should make sure that we are doing it as a service to God. As the work is being done for God's pleasure—not our own—it becomes unselfish work. Performance of unselfish work gradually purifies the mind thus enabling us to see God. This is Karma Yoga.

Japa is work. But what kind of work—selfish or unselfish? As long as spiritual aspirants perform Japa to reach their own spiritual goal, it can be considered selfish, although this selfishness is not the usual kind of selfishness. It is enlightened selfishness. Nevertheless, Hindu tradition instructs us not to perform Japa for selfish reasons, but to do it as a loving service to God. Japa performed in this manner gradually purifies our minds and enables us to have God-vision.

Toward the end of ritualistic worship in the tradition of Tantra, the worshipper is required to do Japa for a while. At the end of the Japa the worshipper takes some water in cupped hands, and using the water as a symbol of Japa, offers it to God. Through this symbolic gesture the results of the spiritual practice are offered to God, thereby transforming the worshipper's Japa into unselfish work. Similarly, we can transform all our secular activities into unselfish ones by mentally offering them to God. This is the technique of spiritualizing secular activities.

Japa leads to Dhyâna and Samâdhi

Spiritual progress happens by stages. Through the practice of Japa we may first reach a lower plateau of spiritual growth. To go to the next higher level we have to further intensify our practice of Japa. In this manner we will eventually arrive at the highest stage, where we will experience God through Samâdhi. It has been said that Japa gradually matures into Dhyâna (meditation), and Dhyâna into Samâdhi. Japa, as a spiritual discipline, is not a watertight compartment; it is complementary to meditation.

Japa is encouraged by Bhakti Yoga, Râja Yoga and Jnâna Yoga

Japa forms a vital part of the Bhakti Yoga and Râja Yoga disciplines. Both prescribe the chanting of the holy name of the Personal God or Îshwara. Jnâna Yoga also encourages its followers to chant Mantras, such as *Soham Hamsah*. This mantra speaks of the identity of the individual soul with Impersonal God or Nirguna Brahman.[3]

Obstacles and problems encountered in the practice of Japa

When spiritual aspirants perform Japa they may encounter the following obstacles and hazards. These are similar to those encountered during meditation.

1. Boredom

After obtaining Siddha Mantras from competent teachers, sincere spiritual aspirants at first find considerable joy in performing Japa. After a while the novelty of practicing Japa starts wearing off, and their minds become reluctant to chant the Mantra. Such reluctance is caused by the natural tendency of the mind to get bored doing the same thing over and over again. Spiritual aspirants must exercise will power to overcome this obstacle. Whether their minds like it or not, they should forcibly persuade their minds to continue doing Japa.

An uncontrolled mind is mischievous. It resents being controlled and invents various tricks to escape the restraints imposed upon it. Let us suppose a spiritual aspirant has been asked by the teacher to chant the Mantra *Shiva*. But the mind gets bored with chanting the same

---

3. See *Nirguna Brahman* in the Glossary

Mantra repeatedly. It may say, "Why should you chant *Shiva* all the time? Why don't you chant the Mantra *Vishnu* for a change? After all, both Mantras imply one and the same God!" If the spiritual aspirant listens to this prompting and acts accordingly, the aspirant will be committing a grave mistake. Rather than gaining control over the mind, the aspirant will end up being controlled by the mind itself. The aspirant should stubbornly stick to the chanting of the holy word Shiva. Eventually the mind will come under control and obey whatever it is ordered to do.

2. Wandering of the mind (Vikshepa)

When people try to perform Japa, their minds sometimes start wandering. To overcome this obstacle they should mentally enunciate the holy name correctly and listen to it intently. That will stop the wandering of the mind.

3. Sleep (Laya)

While performing Japa spiritual aspirants may sometimes be overpowered by a kind of refreshing sleep called Laya. This happens when they are tired. To avoid this obstacle they should perform Japa when not feeling tired or sleepy. There is less likelihood of falling asleep if people practice Japa in the morning after a refreshing sleep. Taking a shower before Japa can be of additional help.

Having a siesta for an hour in the afternoon can prevent Laya during Japa in the evening. However, a siesta for more than an hour will have an adverse effect. It will make the mind more lethargic and prone to falling asleep.

4. Unwelcome thoughts arising in the mind

People practicing Japa often find it hard to concentrate on their Mantras because of unwanted thoughts arising in their minds. For instance, if one had an unpleasant argument with another person, the thought of that unpleasant experience might arise in the mind and disturb the practice of Japa. Such disturbances can be very frustrating. The following techniques can be used to handle this problem:

(a) Solving unresolved daily problems: Once a company executive said to me, "Swâmî, I have set a time in the evening to perform Japa. But most days when I sit to do Japa, the first thoughts arising in my mind are those related to my work, not the holy name of God! How can I get rid of these disturbing thoughts?"

I told him, "It is normal for the most powerful thoughts of the day to arise in your mind when you are trying to calm your mind down and perform Japa. Obviously your strongest thoughts of the day are about your work-related problems. Therefore, they will be the first ones to rise in your mind when you sit for Japa. You are like a person sitting on the bank of a big river and watching a powerful motorboat pass by at great speed. While passing the boat generates big waves in the river. These waves do not hit the bank immediately. They take some time to come and splash against the bank. Similarly, the thoughts of your unresolved work-related problems, which created strong waves in your mind several hours ago, are now hitting your mind as you try to prepare it for Japa. By exercising will power you may try to expel them. If you succeed, well and good! But if you cannot do that, you have to resolve those problems first. Otherwise, it will not be possible for you to perform Japa. Only after solving those problems will it be possible for you to put your mind at rest and perform Japa."

(b) Anticipation of problems and solving them in advance: In Shrî Râmakrishna's life we find the following interesting incident that shows how unwelcome thoughts can be nipped in the bud before they have started disturbing Japa or meditation.

For several years Shrî Râmakrishna's widowed mother lived with him in the village of Dakshineswar near Calcutta. In spite of her old age, like any other Hindu mother, she would insist on cooking his meals and would derive great joy from it. Shrî Râmakrishna, the loving son that he was, tried to help his mother by cutting vegetables every day for her cooking. And he would usually do that in the morning.

At that time Shrî Râmakrishna's nephew Hriday used to live with him. They shared the same bedroom. Once around midnight Hriday woke up and was surprised to see Shrî Râmakrishna busy cutting vegetables at that unearthly hour!

"Uncle, what are you doing?" asked Hriday. "It's midnight! Why are you cutting vegetables now?"

Shrî Râmakrishna replied, "You see, Hriday, when I'll sit for meditation in the early morning, the thought that I've to cut vegetables may come and disturb my meditation. In order to prevent that I'm cutting the vegetables right now!"

(c) Use of positive thoughts to counteract negative thoughts: Not all disturbing thoughts are like the ones experienced by the above company executive or Shrî

Râmakrishna. Some thoughts can be very negative, such as thoughts of anger and hatred. Let us suppose a person had an argument with his wife in the morning. During that argument she made some very cutting remarks which were extremely upsetting to him. Later, as he was driving to work he kept on thinking: "How could she be so cruel? She must not love me anymore! Otherwise, how could she talk to me so harshly?" Even after reaching his office he continues to ruminate over his wife's unpleasant behavior. As a result, by the time he was driving back home after work his mind had become so full of anger, resentment and hatred that he started seriously thinking of divorcing her!

In this disturbed mental state is it possible for him to sit quietly and perform Japa or practice meditation? Obviously not! Unless he gets rid of his anger, it will not be possible for him to do either of them. But how will he get rid of his anger and hatred? The great sage Patanjali comes to his rescue. In his book *Yoga-Sûtras (Aphorisms on Yoga)*, he says, "To obstruct thoughts which are inimical to the practice of Yoga, contrary thoughts should be used."[4]

Swâmî Vivekânanda in his commentary on this aphorism writes, "When a big wave of anger has come into the mind, how are we to control that? Just by raising an opposing wave. Think of love. Sometimes a woman is very angry with her husband, and while in that state, the baby comes in, and she kisses the baby; the old wave dies out and a new wave arises—love for the child. That suppresses the other one. Love is opposite to anger."

---

4. "Vitarka-bâdhane pratipaksha-bhâvanam"—*Yoga-Sûtras*, 2/33.

The angry husband should use contrary thoughts to get rid of his anger and hatred. He should try to think lovingly about his wife. It may be hard, but he should try to remember those happy days when they were first married and how dearly they loved each other. He should try to remember how lovingly she nursed him every time he fell ill. He should try to remember how she gave him sympathy and emotional support whenever he needed them. He should try to recollect how all these years, in spite of occasional disagreements, they have been able to live together as friends and partners, helping and caring for each other and raising their children. He should also realize that throughout their married life she had always behaved lovingly with him, except perhaps, on only a few occasions. This kind of thinking will counteract his angry thoughts and make his mind peaceful and loving. Only then will it be possible for him to perform Japa or do his meditation.

(d) Praying for the wrongdoer: Sometimes you may feel hurt or offended by others. Such feelings can linger on and disturb your mind at the time of Japa or meditation. To get rid of this disturbance, pray for those who have hurt or offended you. Request God to transform them into loving and compassionate souls. This kind of prayer will make your mind peaceful. Then it will be possible for you to do your spiritual practice without disturbance.

I have often met people who consider themselves very sensitive. They easily get hurt or offended by others. A little self-examination will reveal that this sensitivity is self-pity. Those who don't feel the pain of others, and weep and wail only at their own distress—whether imagined or real—are selfish. They are not truly sensitive. On the other hand, those who are truly sensitive weep at other people's distress more than their own.

5. Rejuvenated impressions of past thoughts (Samskâras)

At times while performing Japa, we may notice unwanted thoughts rising in our minds. They may be vulgar, violent or angry thoughts. And we may wonder why these unholy thoughts are coming to us, and it may frighten us. In such a situation it is best for us to seek our teachers' help. From our teachers we will learn that there is no cause for alarm. What is happening is an indication that Japa has started working. Japa causes hidden Samskâras[5] to rise from the subconscious to the conscious level. Samskâras are impressions of past thoughts stored in the subconscious. Some of them can even be thoughts from past incarnations. Depending upon the nature of the past thoughts, Samskâras can be either good or bad.

For mental purification our minds have to get rid of both good and bad Samskâras. Japa helps in cleansing our minds of all the accumulated Samskâras—both good and bad. Such cleansing purifies our minds and enables us to have God-vision.

As one by one the good or bad Samskâras rise to the conscious level, they become live thoughts again. Bad Samskâras rising to the conscious level may manifest themselves as vulgar and violent thoughts, while good Samskâras manifest themselves as good thoughts. This is an indication that Japa has started cleansing our minds of its accumulated Samskâras. If we are performing Japa, we should watch the rejuvenated thoughts like disinterested

---

5. See page 57 to know more about Samskâras

Vijaykrishna Goswâmî
(1841–1899)

observers and not act upon them. If we act upon the rejuvenated thoughts, new Samskâras will be created and the cleansing process through Japa will never be completed. If old thoughts that have reached the conscious level are not acted upon, they will burst like so many air bubbles and disappear, never to return again. This is how Japa, by gradually getting rid of the Samskâras, purifies the mind.

We may not be in a position to determine which thoughts rising in our minds are new thoughts and which are rejuvenated Samskâras. Nevertheless, all thoughts coming up in the mind during Japa, other than the holy name of God (Mantra), should be considered obstacles by spiritual aspirants and must not be acted upon.

Shrî Vîjaykrishna Goswâmî, a 19th century saint of India, described the process of rejuvenation of Samskâras beautifully with the help of an analogy. He compared the mind to a tropical forest. Many wild animals are hidden inside it. They are not usually visible. If somebody sets fire to the forest, all the animals start running out. In this analogy the forest is the subconscious mind and the animals are the hidden Samskâras. One who sets fire to the forest is the Guru. The fire is the Siddha-Mantra, the chanting of which gradually brings out all the hidden Samskâras—good or bad. As a result, the mind becomes pure.

XVIII

JUDGING OUR OWN
SPIRITUAL PROGRESS

The expression *spiritual progress* literally means progress of the spirit. The indwelling spirit or the soul is ever perfect; how can it progress or regress? It is the mind that progresses or regresses. Therefore, in spiritual life the term *spiritual progress* actually means mental progress—it means improvement of the quality of the mind. How can this be measured?

Many who have engaged in spiritual practice for a short while want to know how much progress they have made. Unfortunately, it is not that easy to measure our spiritual growth. It is like measuring the height of a young apple sapling every five minutes to know how much it has grown. Unless a longer time is allowed to elapse between measurements, it will not be possible to notice how much growth has occurred.

The same is true in judging spiritual progress. Progress takes place slowly and almost imperceptibly. We may have to continue doing spiritual practice for years before any tangible progress can be noticed. This is why we need a strong will and great tenacity to persevere. The old unwholesome habits of the mind die hard. These habits, nurtured through many years of indulgence, can be extremely stubborn. To grow spiritually we have to get rid of them completely. Through repeated efforts alone can this be done. New wholesome habits have to be formed to replace the old ones. And it takes time.

Nevertheless, no matter how long it takes to achieve any tangible spiritual progress, this progress can be measured by techniques given by the scriptures. Hindu scriptures like the *Bhagavad Gîtâ* tell us how we can judge our spiritual progress with the help of the knowledge of the Gunas.

The Gunas explain human behavior

Why the same person experiences changing mental states such as happiness, serenity, love, compassion, enthusiasm, false pride, vanity, arrogance, anger, hatred, envy, jealousy, sadness, despondency, confusion and delusion, can be easily explained by the Gunas.[1]

When we are happy, serene, loving and compassionate, it is an indication that our minds at that time have a preponderance of Sattwa. When we are vain, domineering, arrogant, restless, angry, hateful, envious and jealous, Rajas has become dominant in us. When our minds are lethargic, confused, sad, easily angered for no justifiable cause, deluded and unable to comprehend the deeper meaning of the scriptures, vulnerable to sensual impulses and capable of senseless violence, it is to be understood that Tamas has become preponderant in our minds.

A preponderance of Sattwa indicates a mental state conducive to spiritual progress. A state of preponderance of

---

1. To refresh your knowledge of the Gunas please see pages 54–56.

Rajas or Tamas in our minds is not conducive to spiritual growth. From a spiritual point of view, a preponderance of Tamas is the least suitable for spiritual growth. This condition can be overcome by vigorous physical and mental activities of a positive nature. Such activities will first make Rajas preponderant. Then through the practice of meditation and other spiritual disciplines Rajas can be subdued and Sattwa made preponderant.

If a person displays the characteristics of one particular Guna most of the time, his or her behavior can be easily predicted in terms of the characteristics of that Guna. It also means that a good knowledge of the Gunas can enable us to judge the quality of our own minds as well. If most of the time the characteristics of Sattwa-guna are preponderant in us, we can rest assured that our minds have become mostly pure and we have made sufficient spiritual progress.

Signs and symptoms of genuine spiritual progress

An abbot of the Kânchipuram monastery of the Shankara Order in India was well-known for his saintliness. Once a devotee came to him and asked, "Sir, What's the difference between genuine spiritual visions and hallucination?"

The abbot replied, "The difference can be seen in their effects. A person having hallucinations gradually loses touch with reality and turns insane. On the other hand, one who has genuine spiritual visions becomes spiritually illumined."

Psychotic people suffer from various types of fantasy. Among them two are most common—religious fantasy and sexual fantasy. In my life I have met some mentally ill people with religious fantasies. One believed that God had ordained her to teach the world. Another considered himself a reincarnated apostle of Jesus. Both claimed to have heard the voice of God.

Many years ago when I was in India, a young man whom I knew came to see me. He said that he had acquired the power of clairaudience, that he could hear people talking about him miles away. He also said that twice or thrice he had seen Divine Light. He was convinced that these were all genuine spiritual experiences. But I knew that his mother had a history of mental illness and had had to be institutionalized. I was somehow able to persuade the young man to go and see a psychiatrist. The young man got rid of those symptoms after prolonged treatment.

Another mentally disturbed woman used to have visions of Lord Krishna and considered them genuine spiritual experiences. Proper psychiatric treatment eventually helped her to get rid of that fantasy.

The Yoga scriptures say that a spiritual aspirant can have genuine spiritual visions only when the awakened Kundalinî power enters the Sushumnâ channel. There are certain signs and symptoms of the awakening of the Kundalinî. Immediately before its awakening the spiritual aspirant hears a special sound called *Anâhata Dhwani*. This sound is not produced in the atmosphere. It is heard only by the inner spiritual ear, which is the highly purified mind of the spiritual aspirant.

When the awakened Kundalinî starts coursing through the different Chakras toward the Sahasrâra, the spiritual aspirant has various genuine spiritual experiences. For instance, when the Kundalinî rises to the Anâhata Chakra at the heart level, he sees Divine Light, or luminous figures of Divine beings. When the Kundalinî reaches the Vishuddha Chakra at his neck level, he longs to talk and hear only about God. Talk on worldly topics gives him pain. At this stage he only likes the company of those who love God.

Ashta Sâttwika Vikâra

As stated earlier, in order to have God-vision we must have a preponderance of Sattwa Guna. According to Bhakti Yoga, a person with a preponderance of Sattwa Guna may display eight external signs and symptoms. These symptoms, called Ashta Sâttwika Vikâra, are indicative of genuine spiritual progress. The symptoms are (1) shedding tears, (2) profuse perspiration, (3) horripilation, (4) pallor of skin, (5) fainting, (6) shivering of the body, (7) temporary hoarseness of voice and (8) becoming stupefied and speechless. All these symptoms are generated by an intense love of God.

The scriptures say that tears shed out of love of God flow from the outer corners of the eyes, not from the inner corners. Moreover, they have much less salinity than the usual tears. Perspiration caused by intense spiritual emotion can be so profuse that one's shirt may become soaking wet. At the same time, the perspiration will not have an unpleasant odor. Intense love of God may make a person's hair stand on end all over the body. The aspirant's skin may also turn temporarily pale. Sometimes intense spiritual emotions cause a kind of fainting, which is quite different from fainting caused by illness. When a person faints due to illness there is a loss of both inner and outer consciousness. But a person fainting from genuine spiritual emotion retains inner consciousness. The person remains fully conscious of God. Usually intense cold, fear, and anger can cause shivering of the body—which is uncomfortable. But trembling from genuine spiritual emotions is always accompanied by a feeling of joy. Ordinary hoarseness of voice is caused either by excessive talking or by a throat infection, but the hoarseness of voice referred to above is caused by intense spiritual emotion. This symptom disappears when the spiritual emotion subsides. Sometimes heightened spiritual fervor makes the aspirant oblivious of the surroundings. The aspirant becomes like a statue, not communicating with others. The surroundings are forgotten by the aspirant but he or she remains fully conscious of God.

An incident that I witnessed in India many years ago demonstrates this point. At that time Swâmî Yatîswarânanda was the Vice-President of the Râmakrishna Order. He was renowned for his saintliness, and hundreds of devotees used to come to seek his spiritual guidance. One afternoon, at Belur Monastery near Calcutta, some fifty devotees were sitting quietly in the Swâmî's presence in a large room and enjoying his holy company. Finally, a devotee asked the Swâmî, "Revered sir, I have a young son. He seems to be in good health, but sometimes he becomes overwhelmed by a strange mood. He becomes non-responsive and sits like a statue. At that time he doesn't even recognize his father or me. He seems to forget us completely. This condition lasts for a few minutes, then he becomes normal again. We are naturally worried about him. Is this a spiritual state, or a medical condition?"

Swâmî Yatîswarânanda asked in response, "You've told me that he doesn't remember you or your husband at that time, but is there something that he still remembers? Is there something that he doesn't forget?"

The lady replied, "No, sir. He seems to forget everything. He doesn't remember anything."

Thereupon Swâmî Yatîswarânanda said, "Then it's not a spiritual condition. Please take him to a doctor or a psychiatrist." Swâmî Yatîswarânanda knew that had it been a genuine spiritual condition caused by a preponderance of Sattva Guna, the boy might forget everything else, but not God.

XIX

STRESS RELIEF
Through Common Sense and Yoga

Understanding stress

What is stress? In the simplest language it can be described as a lack of mental and physical well-being caused by unpleasant situations or stimuli not under our control. The mind reacts with jealousy, envy, hatred, anger, anxiety, sadness, depression, fear and panic. The mind and body are closely interlinked, and these emotions also adversely affect our physical health. If we cannot manage or prevent these emotions, we start experiencing great physical and mental stress. Unless relieved, such tension may eventually produce serious illnesses, even heart attacks or strokes.

Many consider stress a malady typical of our modern, highly competitive world. They forget that stress existed in prehistoric times as well. The amount of physical and mental stress our cave dwelling ancestors experienced in a single day probably wouldn't be experienced by us even in a year! Yet even today the nervous system of a human body under stress reacts much the same way as it did in the case of our primitive ancestors. Our worry about money or fears of losing our jobs can be just as potent as our primitive ancestors' fears at the sight of prehistoric tigers. Stress can be caused by pleasant situations, as well. For example, having a newborn baby, planning for a pleasure trip or a wedding may cause stress. Be that as it may, we cannot deny that stress is still one of the most pressing problems in today's complicated world.

Stress can be caused by psychological, biological or sociological stimuli. Of the two kinds of stress— mental and physical—mental stress is often the worse. For our physical and psychological survival we have to address this problem, and learn to resolve it effectively. A combination of common sense, rational thinking and Yoga can rescue us. To relieve physical stress, Hatha Yoga postures can be helpful, while the techniques of meditation taught by Râja Yoga can relieve mental stress.

Desire causes stress

Hinduism as well as Buddhism teaches that stressful emotions stem from our cherished desires or longings. When desires are obstructed, they become anger, jealousy, hatred, etc. The following two verses of the *Bhagavad Gîtâ* beautifully express this idea:

> A person who thinks of sense objects develops attachment for them. From this attachment grows desire or longing, and from desire springs anger.

> From anger follows delusion, and from delusion loss of memory. From loss of memory comes the inability to discriminate between what is good and what is bad. From loss of discrimination the person perishes.[1]

---

1. *Bhagavad Gîtâ*—Verses 2/62 & 2/63.

Attachment is attraction to anyone or anything with a selfish motive. Consider a young man who has become attracted to a beautiful girl. The more he thinks of her the stronger grows his attraction. This attraction is attachment. This attachment generates a strong desire in him to possess the girl for his enjoyment. He wants to marry her. But the girl decides to marry someone else. Her rejection of him becomes an obstacle to the fulfillment of his cherished desire. This makes him extremely angry. He becomes so overwhelmed with anger that his thinking gets utterly confused. He becomes deluded. This delusion causes loss of memory. He forgets all the moral and ethical lessons he has learned. He loses the ability to discriminate between right and wrong—what is proper and what is improper. Driven by a blind impulse he gets a gun and kills the man the girl wants to marry. For his crime he is arrested by the police and eventually put to death.

In another example, a very good-looking girl goes to a party. There she meets another girl much more beautiful than she. This makes her jealous because the other girl's presence stands in the way of the fulfillment of her desire to be the most beautiful girl at that party.

Hinduism teaches that negative stress-producing emotions like anger, hatred, envy, jealousy and fear are not essentially different from one another. One emotion easily becomes transformed into another. And all are caused by attachment and desire.

Everyone desires freedom and resents its curtailment. Employees in subordinate positions resent their lack of freedom in making the final decisions. It is the bosses who make such decisions. This resentment causes stress.

For chief executive officers of large companies, stress may be brought on by their inability to perform up to the expectations of the stockholders. If they do not perform satisfactorily, if they cannot show a profit, they will be fired. They find that their desire to work freely is obstructed by the interference of the stockholders. Awareness of their lack of freedom and of being at the mercy of the stockholders makes them resentful. This resentment causes stress.

A Yogic technique to relieve physical stress

One method to relieve stress is to learn to relax your body. Lie on your back on the carpeted floor of your bedroom. Don't use a pillow under your head. You may lie on your bed if the mattress is very firm and will not cause any curvature in your backbone while lying down. Breathe rhythmically for five minutes. Then relax your whole body, thinking that all the joints of your body have become loose. Relax the joints of your feet first, then the knees, then the joints of your arms, and last of all the neck. Lie in that relaxed position for at least fifteen minutes. If you have succeeded, your body will lie limp on the floor. This technique is called Shavâsana in Hatha Yoga. It will often lull you into a restful sleep.

Even when sitting in a straight-back armchair, similar relaxation of the body joint by joint can be practiced. To start with, rest both your arms on the arms of the chair.

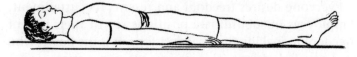

Shavâsana (Corpse Posture)

Your back should be held erect against the back of the chair. First relax the joints of your feet, then your knees, then your arms, and finally your neck. The neck, when relaxed, will not be able to hold your head erect. It will droop and your chin will rest on your chest. This technique should not be practiced for more than ten minutes. Someone having problems with the vertebrae of the neck must not use this technique, but should practice Shavâsana instead.

Techniques to reduce mental stress

Management of emotions: To remove mental stress we should first try to prevent stress-producing emotions from arising in our minds. Nevertheless, if they arise, they have to be handled carefully. Worry causes stress. Worry, anxiety and fear are states of mental apprehension. The disaster has not come, yet its apprehension causes stress. When disaster strikes, we are no longer afraid, anxious or worried. The fears, anxieties and worries caused by the anticipated disaster are gone. Now we are only busy trying to survive.

Even in this changed situation new fears may come. As long as we identify with our body-mind complex, we cannot totally overcome fear. The fear of possible harm to the body and of death may still linger on, causing stress. Total fearlessness comes only from the highest form of Samâdhi, such as Asamprajnâta Samâdhi. In that Samâdhi we acquire the experiential knowledge that we are not the body-mind complex, but are the Eternal Divine Spirit—birthless and deathless. Nevertheless, for those who have not had Samâdhi, relief from some kinds of stress can be achieved by the following methods:

Getting rid of attachment: According to Hindu psychology, stress-producing emotions are caused by attachment. As mentioned earlier, attachment means getting involved with anything in a selfish way. This selfish involvement causes fear, worry and anxiety. Suppose a person in New York is walking down an infamous alley at midnight, carrying an attaché case containing $100,000. In this situation there is a possibility that he or she may be mugged. Will that person be scared of losing the money? The answer can be both "Yes" and "No." If the money being carried is the person's own and if he or she is very much attached to it, the person will surely be afraid of losing it. But if the person is not attached and does not mind losing it, there won't be any fear. *Vairâgya Shatakam*, an ancient book by Yogî Bhartrihari, beautifully expresses this idea. Says Bhartrihari:

> If a person be attached to physical enjoyment,
> he will have the fear of disease.
> If he be attached to his social status
> he will be afraid of losing it.
> If he be attached to his wealth
> he will fear the hostile kings
> who may snatch it away.
> If he be attached to honor
> he will be afraid of humiliation.
> If he be attached to power
> he will fear his enemies
> who may render him powerless.
> If he be attached to his beauty
> he will fear his old age.
> If he be attached to his scholarship
> he will fear those who may challenge his
> erudition.

If he be attached to his good reputation
he will fear the wicked who may defame him.
If he be attached to his body
he will be afraid of death.
All the things of the world pertaining to man
are fraught with fear.
Renunciation of attachment alone
causes fearlessness.[2]

By eliminating the attachments mentioned above, many kinds of fear can be overcome. Yet, the fear of death caused by attachment to the body is hard to dispel. But, if we think deeply, we shall realize that the fear of death is also caused by attachment to sense pleasure. We enjoy sensual pleasures—beautiful sights, delicious food, tactile pleasures, sweet music, and fragrances—through our bodies. We need our bodies to enjoy these things. As long as we desire these pleasures, we shall remain attached to our bodies. This is why the thought of losing the body makes us afraid.

Consider someone who has completely lost his or her eyesight, hearing, the ability to smell or taste, and the sensation of touch. That person is incapable now of enjoying the pleasures of sight, sound, smell, taste and touch. The body has become completely useless. In this situation the attachment to the body will be vastly diminished. Such a person may even pray for death to come quickly to end that pleasureless existence.

To get rid of attachment it is helpful to develop a realistic view of the world. There are two worlds—the "should

---

2. *Vairâgya Shatakam* by Bhartrihari—Verse 31. Translated from the original Sanskrit text by the author.

be" world and the "as is" world. The "should be" world is the perfect world of our expectations. It is the Utopia of our imagination, a perfect world that will never come. The "as is" world is the less than perfect world in which we actually live. Judging by societal conditions, only a world devoid of selfishness can be a truly perfect world. Selfishness causes attachment. As long as selfishness dwells in the hearts of people, this ideally perfect "should be" world will never come.

In this less than perfect "as is" world, we have to learn to put up with imperfection for our psychological survival. Moreover, the concept of perfection varies from person to person. It is thus not possible for each of us to change the world to make it match our individual ideas of perfection. We have to accept the world as it is. As no one else is under our complete control, all that we can do is to try to make ourselves better by becoming less selfish and less attached. To that extent, we shall create a more peaceful, stress-free life for ourselves, and the world will also be a better place to live in.

Managing stress through rational thinking

Once a relatively new member of our church came to see me. She had a tendency to take offence easily. I could see that she was quite agitated. I asked her, "What happened? Are you all right?"

She replied, "No I'm not! That's why I've come to talk to you. I've come to tell you that I'm not coming to your church ever again! Nobody ever greets me when I come to this church. What kind of church is this? Members don't seem to have any love for each other!"

I asked her, "Do you greet others when you come here?"

"Why should I? Aren't they supposed to greet me first to make me feel welcome?" she argued.

"Others may also think like you," I said, "they may expect you to greet them first." My counter-argument only made her all the more agitated. She blamed me for being biased, unfair and insensitive, and angrily left my office without even saying "Good bye." It was obvious that she was upset and under stress. But a little rational thinking could have saved her from this. Let me cite a few more cases to drive my point home.

Once another member of our church, a lady, came to my office in an agitated mood and said, "I told my husband today, 'You don't love me anymore!'"

I said to her, "Why did you say such a thing? It is quite possible that he still loves you. In that case, won't your words upset him? On the other hand, if he really doesn't love you, isn't he the first person to know? Does he need to be told that he doesn't love you? You can't force anyone to love you by demanding love. A better method to regain his love would have been to give him more love and care in a manner that he would understand and appreciate. Even animals respond to love, why not a human being?"

There are some people who readily take offence at the slightest provocation. For flimsy reasons they terminate their relationships with friends and relatives. At the same time, they nurture hatred and anger for years towards those they have shunned. Like smoldering fires, these sustained negative feelings keep on causing them stress. Their withdrawal from people they don't like causes their world to gradually shrink and become a little shell—a self-created prison. The consequence is terrible loneliness and mental depression. A little rational thinking can come to their rescue. They should understand that it is unrealistic to expect others to always give them what they want, such as endless attention, love, praise and appreciation. Relationships between people are a two-way traffic. People expect reciprocity. To get love and attention, one should give love and attention to others. Behaving like a black hole and expecting that attention, love, praise and appreciation from others will continually flow in and never go out is totally unrealistic. Such thinking only invites stress in the form of many kinds of psychological and physical sufferings.

Getting rid of stress through positive comparisons

Comparisons can cause either happiness or unhappiness. The kind of comparison that causes unhappiness may be called negative comparison. The kind that causes happiness may be called positive comparison. Positive comparison can help in getting rid of psychological stress.

One gentleman had developed the habit of feeling miserable most of the time. His miserable feelings were largely caused by negative comparisons such as, "My brother is very successful in life and I'm not; all my neighbors have nicer and bigger homes while my home is the smallest; my friends' sons are extremely gifted and enterprising but my sons are not," etc. He felt so miserable and depressed that he would often speak of death. But once he had to go and see a patient in a hospital. There he saw several young people paralyzed from various sport-related accidents. Some were quadriplegic. They were unable to move their legs and arms. And these young men were expected to live that way for many more years. This experience opened the eyes of that gentleman. Through positive comparison—comparing his own condition with that of the paralyzed patients—he suddenly realized how lucky he was. He shook off his miserable feelings and started volunteering as a nurse's aid in that hospital. This selfless service gave him great joy and satisfaction.

The support group concept used by organizations like Alcoholics Anonymous is based on positive comparison.

Managing stress through meditation

Meditation, if practiced properly, can effectively relieve physical and mental stress. To know about meditation please see Chapters X, XI and XII.

Preparing for the worst and trying to prevent it from happening

Much mental stress is caused by the anticipation of unwanted events. To manage this kind of stress, it helps to mentally assess the worst that can happen and then prepare for its prevention. In reality most anticipated events never take place. Yet, knowing the worst that can happen and being prepared for it can greatly reduce stress. For example, during the Second World War Londoners feared that their city would be bombed. Many were panic-stricken. Meanwhile, various precautionary measures were taken, such as building air-raid shelters all over the city, introducing daily blackouts, training people to respond to air-raid sirens, and forming Air Raid Precaution (A.R.P) units all over London. Citizens were also educated about the harm bombings could cause and how to protect themselves from bombing raids. In short, Londoners were made fully prepared psychologically and otherwise for that

eventuality. As a result, panic-related stress was vastly
diminished.

XX

CONCLUDING REMARKS

Those practicing meditation and other techniques for controlling the mind often lose interest in their practice. Or worse, they give up their practice altogether because they do not get any tangible, quick results. Why they notice no perceptible result may have more than one cause.

Firstly, they do not realize that fulfilling the ethical and moral requirements are essential for achieving tangible results. A mind not strengthened through moral and ethical exercises is easily distracted by the lure of sense objects. Such a mind naturally resists concentration.

Secondly, very few want to study their minds and find the hidden defects. The average person's mind is like the rug in a living room. Over the years a lot of dust accumulates under the rug, but the dirt remains completely hidden. Nobody can see it. Similarly, the typical human mind also has many hidden defects. Before an important guest's visit, the housewife thoroughly cleans her home. She dusts the furniture, vacuums the rugs, and even removes cobwebs from the walls and ceilings of her house. But she feels no urge to clean under the living room rug because the dust will not be seen by the guest. So also are the defects hidden in a person's mind. The defects are not visible to others. Thus, there is no urgency to eliminate them. To improve the quality of the mind, however, elimination of these defects is absolutely necessary.

Aside from that, all seem to have a special sympathy for themselves. This sympathy, caused by self-love, makes it difficult for them to notice their own defects. On the other hand, they easily notice other people's defects because they lack that same sympathy for others. This is another reason why people do not have the urge to eliminate their own defects.

Spiritual progress mainly consists in first discovering the defects hidden in the mind, and then effectively eliminating them. Only minds completely cleansed of defects can meditate properly and achieve Samâdhi.

Patanjali again draws our attention to another important fact. He states, "Success in Yoga is speedy for the extremely energetic."[1] He also says, "The flow of the continuous control of the mind becomes steady when practiced regularly day after day."[2] In other words, enthusiasm and regularity in practice are essential.

The *Yoga-Sûtras* also makes the very striking point that the goal of meditation can be achieved by devotional practices as well. In other words, there is no conflict between Râja Yoga and Bhakti Yoga.

The Hindu scriptures say that there cannot be an action that does not produce any effect. In other words, every good effort must produce a beneficial effect. Therefore, those who practice Yoga need not be disheartened; they

---

1. *Yoga-Sûtras*, 1/21.
2. Ibid., 3/10.

are bound to succeed. The *Bhagavad Gîtâ* says that one who does good deeds will never suffer from any bad consequences. Shrî Râmakrishna assures the devotees that God comes ten steps towards a devotee who has walked only one step towards God. All that a student of Yoga has to do is to practice regularly under the guidance of a proper teacher.

Finally, students of meditation should again be reminded that the purpose of Yoga is not to acquire supernatural powers, but to experience divinity. This is the highest goal of spiritual life. By attaining it, one becomes perfect, immortal and satisfied forever.

APPENDIX A

Meditation, Samâdhi, and enlightenment shown through pictures & sculpture

Buddha in meditation

There are many sculptures depicting Lord Buddha in meditation. This is one of them. The sculpture shows that he has withdrawn his mind from the external world and has concentrated it within.

Swâmî Vivekânanda in meditation

This photograph shows Swâmî Vivekânanda in meditation. The photograph was taken during his visit to London in 1896.

Shrî Loknâth Brahmachârî in meditation

Shrî Loknâth Brahmachârî (1729–1890) was a contemporary of Shrî Râmakrishna. He was a renowned Yogi who lived in the village of Barodi in Bengal. The drawing is based on a photograph that shows him practicing a form of meditation which involves concentrating his gaze on the tip of his nose. This is a technique taught by some Yoga books.

The Holy Mother Shrî Sâradâ Devî

As arranged by Sister Niveditâ (Margaret Noble) and Sara Bull, this photograph of the Holy Mother Shrî Sâradâ Devî was taken professionally in Calcutta in November 1898. While the picture was being taken she entered into Bhâva Samâdhi. Her indrawn gaze indicates that she was not seeing anything outside; her entire mind at that time was in communion with God.

Shrî Râmakrishna in Bhâva Samâdhi

This photograph of Shrî Râmakrishna was taken in Mr. Keshab Sen's house in Calcutta after he entered into Bhâva Samâdhi. His nephew Hriday is holding up Shrî Râmakrishna's body to prevent it from slumping to the floor. In this kind of Bhâva Samâdhi Shrî Râmakrishna would commune with God and lose his body consciousness. This often caused his body to collapse on the floor.

Shrî Râmakrishna in the deepest Samâdhi

A professional photographer took this photograph of Shrî Râmakrishna in the Kâlî Temple in Dakshineswar, Calcutta. When the picture was taken Shrî Râmakrishna was immersed in the deepest Samâdhi, as was acknowledged by Shrî Râmakrishna himself when the photograph was shown to him later.

Monk at the moment of enlightenment
Used with the permission of the Seattle Art Museum

This Chinese sculpture in polychromed wood is from the Yuan Dynasty (1279-1368). It depicts the exuberant joy of freedom enjoyed by the monk. At the moment of enlightenment the monk has acquired freedom from all kinds of suffering—the ultimate spiritual goal to be achieved in Buddhism.

APPENDIX B

Recommended Reading

Râja Yoga by Swâmî Vivekânanda, Ramakrishna-Vivekananda Center, New York, 1982

Yoga Philosophy of Patanjali by Swâmî Hariharânanda Âranya, Motitlal Banarsidass, 2000

An Introduction to Indian Philosophy by S. Chatterjee and D. Datta, Motitlal Banarsidass, 1984

Outlines of Indian Philosophy by M. Hiriyanna, Motitlal Banarsidass, 2000

Fundamentals of Indian Philosophy by R. Puligandla, Motitlal Banarsidass, 1997

The Gospel of Sri Ramakrishna translated by Swâmî Nikhilânanda, Ramakrishna-Vivekananda Center, 2000

The Essentials of Hinduism by Swami Bhaskarananda, Viveka Press, 1994

GLOSSARY

– A –

Abhyâsa: Practice

Abhinivesha: Blind clinging to life.

Agni: The fire-element.

Agni-arka-vishâdinâm pratishtambha: The power not to be affected by fire, water and poison.

Ahankâra: Ego/egoism.

Ajnâna: Ignorance of Divinity.

Âjnâ: *See* Âjnâ Chakra

Âjnâ Chakra: One of the spiritual levels attained through the practice of Yoga. *See also* Kundalinî

Âkâsha: The sky-element.

Akhanda Japa: Continuous chanting of the holy name for a specified period.

Akhanda Nâma Sankîrtana: Singing the holy name continuously for a specified period.

Ajapâ Japa: Automatic chanting of the holy name.

Alabdha-bhûmikatwa: Non-attainment of any level of concentration.

Âlasya: Lethargy.

Anâhata: A sound which is not produced by any vibration in the atmosphere. Only advanced Yogis or spiritual aspirants can hear this sound with their mental ears.

Anâhata Chakra: A level of spiritual consciousness. *See also* Kundalinî

Anâhata Dhwani: *See* Anâhata

219

Anavasthitatwa: Inability to retain a level of concentration once attained.

Anga-mejayatwa: Involuntary nervous trembling of the body— an obstacle to the practice of Yoga.

Animâ: The ability to become as small as a molecule and penetrate solid objects.

Antahkarana: The inner instrument that helps us to know things. Although a technical word, it roughly means the mind.

Antardhânam: The Yogic power to become invisible.

Anurmi-mattwam: The Yogic power to overcome hunger and thirst.

Ap: The water-element.

Apâna: The energy responsible for eating, drinking, voiding and procreation.

Arjuna: A heroic prince of the *Mahâbhârata* who was the son of King Pându and a friend and student of Shrî Krishna.

Asamprajnâta Samâdhi: Concentration par excellence. It is the highest spiritual level attainable through the practice of Yoga.

Âsana: The third step prescribed in Râja Yoga—a sitting posture.

Âsana-Siddha: One who has mastered a Yoga posture.

Asang-sakti: A spiritual level that can be attained through the practice of Yoga.

Ashrama: A hermitage where monks or nuns live.

Ashta sâttwika vikâra: Eight symptoms of enhanced spirituality.

Asmitâ: Egoism.

Asmitâ Samâdhi: The highest level of Samprajnâta Samâdhi.

Avidyâ: A term of Vedânta philosophy meaning ignorance.
   See also Ajnâna

Avirati: The reluctance to give up sense pleasure.

Ayama: Control.

– B –

Shrîmad Bhâgavatam: One of the Puranas. It is a scripture of Hinduism.

Bhagavad Gîta: A well-known Hindu scripture that forms a part of the *Mahâbhârata,* a Hindu epic.

Bhakti Yoga: The Path of Love; one of the four fundamental types of spiritual discipline.

Bhâva Samâdhi: A kind of Samâdhi achieved through devotion.

Bhaya-bhairava: The terrible fear experienced by some spiritual aspirants.

Bîja-Mantra(s): The sacred syllable(s), signifying God.

Brahmânanda Keshab Chandra Sen: A 19th century leader of the Brâhmo Samâj church of India. *See also* Keshab Chandra Sen

Brahma-vid-vara: A knower of Brahman superior to a Brahma-vit.

Brahma-vid-variân: A knower of Brahman superior to a Brahma-vid-vara.

Brahma-vid-varishtha: A knower of Brahman superior to a Brahmavid-variân.

Brahma-vit: A knower of Brahman (God).

Brâhmo Samâj: A reformist church in Hinduism.

Bhîma: A son of King Pandu.

Bhrânti-darshana: False knowledge.

Buddha: The founder of Buddhism. Also considered a Divine Incarnation in Hinduism.

Buddhism: A religion that is an offshoot of Hinduism. It is atheistic and sets the goal of spiritual life as complete cessation of misery. The founder of this religion is Gautama Buddha.

– C –

Chaitanya Mahâprabhu (1485-1533): A great Hindu saint of Bengal. He is also considered a Divine Incarnation by many.

Celibacy: Abstinence.

Chakras: Spiritual levels attained through the practice of Yoga.

Chetana Samâdhi: A kind of Samâdhi usually achieved through devotion.

Chidâkâsha: "Knowledge" space.

Chittâkâsha: "Mental" space.

– D –

Daurmanasya: Despair.

Deva-krîdânudarshanam: The ability to enjoy the celestial pleasures of the gods and angels.

Dhâranâ: The sixth step to Yoga as prescribed by Patanjali—fixing the mind on a single object after withdrawing it from everything else.

Dhyâna: Also called meditation. This is the seventh step to Yoga as prescribed by Patanjali. Dhyâna is a state of uninterrupted concentration of the mind on a single object.

Divine Essence: Formless Divinity permeating in and through everything.

Divine Incarnation: God incarnated on earth assuming a physical form.

Divine Mother Durgâ: A name of the Divine Mother. (The Divine Mother is God looked upon as mother)

Divine Mother Kâlî: One of the many names of the Divine Mother.

Drona: An ancient teacher of martial art mentioned in the *Mahabharata*, a Hindu epic.

Duhkha: Suffering–both mental and physical.

Dûra-darshanam: The ability to see with Yogic power what is happening far away, beyond the ordinary range of seeing.

Dûra-shravanam: The ability to hear with Yogic power what is being said far away, beyond the ordinary range of hearing.

Dwesha: Aversion.

– E –

Edison, Thomas A.: Famous American inventor.

– G –

Gaudiya Vaishnava: Follower of a particular sect of Vaishnavism.

Gomukhâsana: One of the sitting postures taught by Hatha Yoga.

Guna: Property or characteristic trait; any of the three subtle substances that constitute Prakriti or Mother Nature. According to Sânkhya philosophy, Prakriti consists of three Gunas known as Sattva, Rajas, and Tamas. Tamas stands for inertia or dullness, Rajas for activity or restlessness, Sattva for balance, harmony or righteousness.

Guru: Spiritual teacher. Also one who gives secular education.

– H –

Hatha-Yoga: A school of Yoga that aims chiefly at physical health and well-being.

Hinduism: One of the most ancient of the major religions. It is practiced mainly in India.

Hriday Bhattâchârya: A nephew of Shrî Râmakrishna.

– I –

Idâ: The left channel inside the backbone.

Îshitwa: Acquiring godlike powers.

Îshwara-pranidhâna: Surrender to God.

– J –

Jada Samâdhi: A state of most intense concentration of the mind on a single object. Also known as Nirvikalpa Samâdhi or Asamprajnata Samâdhi.

Jainism: An offshoot of Hinduism. It is one of the major world religions and is practiced mainly in India.

Japa: Repetition of a holy name.

Jesus Christ: The founder of Christianity.

Jîvanmukta: One who has become liberated even while alive.

Jnâna Yoga: The Path of Knowledge—one of the four fundamental types of spiritual discipline.

Jnânendriya: Any one of the five sense organs, such as the organs of sight, hearing, smelling, tasting, and touching.

– K –

Kâma-rüpam: The ability to transform the body into any other desired physical form.

Kâma-vasâyitâ: The ability to obtain whatever one desires.

Karma Yoga: The Path of Right Action—one of the four fundamental types of spiritual discipline.

Kânchipuram: A holy city in South India.

Karmendriya: Any of the five motor organs, such as the vocal organ, arms, legs, the organ of elimination, and the organ of reproduction.

Kashâya: Dryness of mind causing a great reluctance to spiritual practice.

Kathâ Upanishad: One of the holy books of Hinduism.

Kaushika: The name of an ascetic mentioned in the Hindu epic Mahâbhârata.

Keshab Chandra Sen: A renowned leader of the Brahmo Samaj church, and the founder of its branch, the "Navabidhân."

Khecharî-vidyâ: The power to fly.

Krishna: According to Hinduism, an Incarnation of God.

Kshiti: According to Hinduism, the element called "earth."

Kundalî; A coil.

Kundalinî power: The dormant spiritual power of man that resides between the base of the sexual organ and the anus. When awakened through spiritual practice, it enters the Sushumnâ channel that is inside the backbone and starts coursing upward toward the brain. Inside the Sushumnâ channel there are six different centers of spiritual awareness called Chakras. They are, in ascending order: (1) Mûlâdhâra, (2) Svâdhishthâna, (3) Manipura, (4) Anâhata, (5) Vishuddha and (6) Âjnâ. These Chakras are visualized by the Yogîs as so many lotuses. The Mûlâdhâra Chakra, situated near the anus, is a four-petaled lotus. The Svâdhishthâna Chakra, situated at the base of the sexual organ, has six petals. The Manipura Chakra, which is in the region of the navel, is a ten-petaled lotus. The Anâhata Chakra, located in the region of the heart, contains twelve petals. The Vishuddha Chakra, near the base of the throat, has sixteen petals. The Âjnâ Chakra, situated between the two eyebrows, is a two-petaled lotus. Mûlâdhâra is the seat of the Kundalinî power. After being awakened, this power passes through these six Chakras and reaches the cerebrum where the Sahasrâra, the thousand-petaled lotus is located. The Sahasrâra is the seat of God (Shiva). When the awakened Kundalinî power reaches the Sahasrâra, the spiritual aspirant becomes illumined.

– L –

Laghimâ: Extreme lightness of the body or the ability to levitate.

Laya: The sleep that comes to a meditator and is an obstacle to meditation.

Lesha Avidyâ: Trace of ignorance.

Likhita Japa: A method of Japa in which the holy name is written and not articulated.

Loknâth Brahmachârî (1729-1890): A Hindu saint who spent his last years in the village of Barodi in East Bengal.

– M –

Mahâbhârata: A Hindu epic.

Mahâbhûtas: The five gross elements: Âkâsha, Vâyu, Agni, Ap and Kshiti.

Mahâkâsha: Outer space.

Mahat: Cosmic intellect.

Mahâvâyu: The awakened Kundalinî power.

Mahendranâth Datta: A younger brother of Swâmî Vivek-ânanda. He was a great scholar and a saintly soul.

Mahimâ: The ability to make the body extremely large.

Manas: Mind.

Mânasa Japa: Chanting of the holy name mentally without generating any audible sound.

Manasija: Lust. This Sanskrit word literally means *something born in the mind.*

Manipura: One of the spiritual levels attainable through the practice of Yoga.

Manipura Chakra: *See* Manipura

Mano-javitwam: The ability to move the body as fast as the speed of the mind.

Mantra: A sacred formula to be uttered in connection with rituals; also a set of holy words.

Mrityunjaya-vidyâ: The power to conquer death.

Mûlâdhâra: The Chakra, located near the lower extremity of the backbone, where the spiritual power of human beings lies dormant. It is also the lowest spiritual level. *See also* Kundalinî

Mûlâdhâra: Chakra. *See* Mûlâdhâra

Mundaka Upanishad: One of the sacred books of Hinduism.

– N –

Nakula: One of the five sons of King Pându.

Nirguna Brahman: Impersonal God; God without any attributes. If we ask, "Who was there before creation?" then the logical reply will be that only the creator, or God, was there. But if we ask, "What was God like before creation?" then Hinduism's reply will be that God was in a transcendental state of existence before creation. The word *transcendental* means that God's existence was beyond time, space and causation.

To make this idea clear, let us take the help of an analogy. Let us consider a person who has fallen asleep and is dreaming. In his dream world, he exists in dream space and dream time, both of which he created with his mind when he created his dream world. He no longer belongs to the time and space of his waking state. In his dream state he has transcended the time and space of his waking state. In the same manner, God's pre-creation existence must have been transcendental existence, in the sense that God then did not belong to the time and space pertaining to this world. The existence of God in that state may be called the True State of Existence of God. In that state God is beyond all limitations imposed by time, space and causation. God in that transcendental state is eternal, infinite and changeless.

In Hinduism, God in this transcendental state of existence is called *Nirguna Brahman,* the Supreme Spirit, the Supreme Brahman, or the Impersonal and Attributeless God. (The Sanskrit word, *Brahman,* literally means *the greatest*) Nirguna Brahman cannot have a personality. Personality is a limitation. Being devoid of a personality, Brahman is also beyond sex. Neither the pronoun *He* nor *She* can be used to denote Brahman. The Vedic scriptures use the Sanskrit neuter pronoun *Tat,* the English counterpart of That, indicating that Brahman is neither male nor female. Transcending space, Brahman is Infinite; transcending time, Brahman is Timeless or Eternal; free from the ceaseless change generated by causation, Brahman is Changeless. Attribute or quality is a factor of separation. For example, the power of burning is a quality of fire. It separates fire from water, which lacks that quality. As Brahman is One, Indivisible and Infinite, It cannot accommodate any kind of separation within Itself. Therefore, Brahman must be attributeless, or free from all qualities.

Hinduism also uses the expressions *Absolute Truth, Consciousness,* and *Infinite Bliss* to mean Brahman. But no matter what epithets are used, Brahman can never be adequately described by the finite words and expressions of our world of limitations. Brahman is indescribable. The great Hindu saint and philosopher Sankaracharya says that Vedic statements such as *Brahman is Eternal Existence, Absolute Knowledge and Infinite Bliss,* are only hints about the nature of Brahman. They are never the description of Brahman.

Nirvichâra Samâdhi: A kind of Samprajnâta Samâdhi.

Nirvikalpa Samâdhi: A super-conscious state during which the aspirant realizes his absolute oneness with the Universal Spirit or Nirguna Brahman.

Nirvitarka Samâdhi: A kind of Samprajnâta Samâdhi.

Niyama: The second step in the course of moral disciplines prescribed by Râja Yoga to cultivate good habits.

– O –

Ojas: According to Hinduism, this is the highest form of energy present in human beings. It is stored up in the brain.

Om: The most sacred word of the Vedas, also written as Aum. It is a symbol of God.

– P –

Padârthâ-bhâvinî: A Yoga level.

Padmâsana: A sitting posture.

King Pându: An ancient king of a kingdom in northern India mentioned in the *Mahâbhârata,* a Hindu epic.

Parachittâdi-abhijnatâ: The ability to read the thoughts of others.

Para-kâya-praveshanam: The Yogic power to enter another person's body.

Paramahamsa: A saint of exalted spirituality. The word literally means the mythological *supreme swan* which can separate milk from a mixture of milk and water. A saint who is a Paramahamsa has the ability to recognize the Real by eliminating the unreal.

Pâtâla-siddhi: One of the supernatural powers which come to a Yogi.

Patanjali: A renowned sage of ancient India who lived in the 2nd Century BC. He is the founder of the Yoga system of Hindu philosophy and the author of the *Yoga Sûtras*.

Pingalâ: The right channel in the spinal column.

Prâkâmya: The acquisition of irresistible will power.

Prakriti: Primordial Nature, in association with Purusha, creates the universe. It is one of the categories in the school of Sânkhya philosophy.

Pramâda: Delusion. It is considered an obstacle to the practice of Yoga.

Prâna: The vital energy. It also means the cosmic energy.

Pranava: The holy syllable Om of Hinduism. *See also* Om

Prânâyâma: A kind of breathing exercise helpful in gaining mental concentration.

Pratyâhâra: The fourth step prescribed by Râja Yoga that teaches the process of withdrawing the mind from sense objects.

Purusha: (lit., a man): A term of Sânkhya philosophy denoting the eternal Sentient Principle. According to Sânkhya there are many Purushas.

Pûrvajâti-jnânam: The Yogic power to remember one's past incarnation/incarnations.

– R –

Râga: Attachment.

Râja Yoga: The Path of Mental Concentration. One of the four fundamental types of spiritual disciplines.

Rajas: One of the three subtle substances constituting Prakriti or Mother Nature.

Râmakrishna: A 19th century Hindu saint (1836-1886) known as the saint of the harmony of religions; also regarded as a Divine Incarnation by many.

Râmakrishna Mission: A philanthropic organization in India named after Shrî Râmakrishna and founded by Swâmî Vivekânanda in 1897.

Ramana Maharshi: A renowned Hindu saint of 20th century India.

Rasâ-Swâda: One of the obstacles to meditation.

– S –

Sâdhakas: Spiritual aspirants.

Saguna Brahman: Brahman with attributes. Impersonal God seen through Mâyâ as the Personal God; the Creator, Preserver, and Destroyer of the universe.

Sahadeva: One of the sons of King Pându.

Sahasrâra: The thousand-petalled lotus in the cerebrum. See also Kundalinî

Sahasrâra Chakra: The highest Yoga level which gives spiritual enlightenment.

Samâdhi: Mental concentration par excellence.

Samâna: The energy that helps in digestion.

Samprajnâta Samâdhi: A kind of Samâdhi inferior to Asamprajnâta Samâdhi.

Samshaya: Doubt.

Samskâras: Impressions of past thoughts.

Samyama: Control/Concentration.

Sânanda Samâdhi: A level of Samprajnâta Samâdhi.

Sânkhya School: The most ancient school of philosophy in India.

Sânkhya System: The school of Sânkhya philosophy.

Sanskrit: An ancient language of India, like Latin, which is no longer spoken. It is the mother of most of the languages in India today. The Hindu scriptures were all written in Sanskrit.

Savitarka Samâdhi: A lower level of Samprajnâta Samâdhi.

Sârada Devî: A renowned woman saint of India (1853—1920). She was the wife of Shrî Râmakrishna.

Sarvabhûtaruta-jnânam: The power to understand the languages of all animals.

Sattâ-patti: A spiritual level attained through the practice of Yoga.

Sattwa: One of the three primordial subtle substances constituting Mother Nature or Prakriti.

Sattwa Guna: Same as above.

Satya-rakshâ: The practice of speaking the truth.

Satya-vâditâ: The truthfulness of one who is established in truth. Whatever such a person says comes true.

Shankara Order: The monastic Order started by Shrî Shankarâchârya.

Shavâsana: A posture in Hatha Yoga.

Shiva: One of the Hindu Trinity representing God as the Destroyer.

Shwâsa-prashwâsa-vikshepa: Irregular breathing and an obstacle to the practice of Yoga.

Shraddhâ: Implicit faith in one's teacher or other respected people.

Shrî Chaitanya Mahâprabhu: *See* Chaitanya Mahâprabhu

Shri Krishna: *See* Krishna

Shrî Râmakrishna: *See* Râmakrishna

Shrî Ramana Maharshi: *See* Ramana Maharshi

Shrî Sârada Devî: *See* Sârada Devî

Shrî Tailanga Swâmî (Circa 1737-1887): A renowned saint of India who spent the major part of his life in the holy city of Banaras.

Shrî Vijaykrishna Goswâmî: *See* Vijaykrishna Goswami

Shubhech-chhâ: One of the spiritual levels attained through the practice of Yoga.

Siddhâsana: A sitting posture in Hatha Yoga.

Siddhi(s): Supernatural power(s). Also means success in achieving the goal of spiritual life.

Sthita Samâdhi: Another name for Asamprajnâta/Nirvikalpa Samâdhi.

Styâna: Lack of interest in spiritual practice. Considered an obstacle to the practice of Yoga.

Sufism: One of the offshoots of Islam.

Sushumnâ: The central narrow channel inside the backbone mentioned in Patanjali's Yoga.

Swâdhishthâna: One of the spiritual levels reached through the practice of Yoga. *See also* Kundalinî

Swâdhishthâna Chakra: *See* Swâdhishthâna

Swâdhyâya: Study of the scriptures.

Swâmî: An ordained Hindu monk who has taken his final vows of renunciation.

Swâmî Vivekânanda (1863-1902): The foremost disciple of Shrî Râmakrishna and the founder of the Râmakrishna Order of monks and the Râmakrishna Mission. He was the first to effectively preach Hinduism in the West. A great orator, he was the star speaker at the Parliament of Religions held in Chicago in 1893.

Swâmî Yatîswarânanda: A monk of the Ramakrishna Order. He was a Vice-President of the Order.

Swechchha-mrityuh: The Yogic power to die at will.

– T –

Tailanga Swâmî: *See* Shrî Tailanga Swamî

Taittiriya Upanishad: One of the sacred scriptures of Hinduism.

Tamas: One of the three subtle substances constituting Prakriti or Mother Nature.

Tanmâtra(s): The elementary constituents of the universe. Tanmatras are extremely subtle.

Tantra: A class of Hindu scriptural texts, not derived directly from the Vedas, presenting God as Shiva and Shakti. Tanumânasâ: One of the Yoga levels.

Trikâlajnatwam: The Yogic power of knowing the past, present and the future.

Tulasi Das (1646-1737): A renowned saint of North India. He authored the *Râmcharit Mânas*.

Turyagâ: The highest level in Yoga.

– U –

Udâna: The vital energy that is used in talking and singing.

Uddhava: A devotee of Shrî Krishna.

Unmanâ Samâdhi: Suddenly withdrawing the mind from the external world and with the greatest concentration focussing on God within.

Upângshu Japa: Chanting the holy name in a whisper.

Upekshâ: The practice of indifference.

– V –

Vâchika Japa: Chanting the holy name audibly.

Vairâgya: The spirit of renunciation. It also means dispassion toward sense pleasures.

Vairâgya Shatakam: A book authored by the sage Bhartrihari.

Vajrâsana: A sitting posture in Hatha Yoga.

Vashitwa: The power to bring everything under one's control.

Vâyu: Air element.

Vedântasâra: A book on Advaita Vedânta (Non-dualistic Vedânta) authored by Sadânanda Yogîndra.

Vichâ-ranâ: One of the Yoga levels.

Vîjaykrishna Goswâmî (1841-1899): Once a renowned leader of the Brahmo Samaj Church, he later dissociated himself from it and became a saint after adopting traditional Hinduism.

Vikshepa: Wandering or restlessness of the mind that is one of the obstacles to meditation and Japa.

Vishnu: The Deity personifying the preserver aspect of God.

Vîrâsana: A sitting posture in Hatha Yoga.

Vishuddha Chakra: One of the Yoga levels. *See* Kundalinî

Vivekananda, Swami: *See* Swami Vivekananda

Vyâdhi: Disease–either mental or physical.

Vyâpti: The ability to permeate everything.

Vyâna: The energy that causes the blood and other vital fluids to circulate throughout the body.

Vy-utthâna: Awakening from Samâdhi.

– Y –

Yama: A preliminary course of moral discipline prescribed in Râja Yoga to restrain harmful thoughts and impulses. Also means the king of death.

Yathâ-samkalpa-samsiddhi: The ability to fulfill one's desires.

Yatîswarânanda, Swâmî: *See* Swâmî Yatîswarânanda

Yoga: (lit., union with God); any course of spiritual discipline that makes for such union.

Yoga-Sutras: A book on Yoga authored by the sage Patanjali. The word literally means *aphorisms on Yoga.*

Yogî: One who practices Yoga.

Yudhistira: The eldest son of King Pându.

INDEX

A

Abhinivesha *107, 110–111*
Abhyâsa *80*
Agni *136*
  See also Mahâ-bhûtas
Agni-arka-vishâdinâm pratishtambhatâ *120*
Ahankâra *134*
Air (element) *136*
  See also Mahâ-bhûtas
Ajapâ Japa *169–170*
  See also Japa
Âjnâ Chakra *125–126*
Âjnâ-apratihata *120*
Âkâsha *136*
  See also Mahâ-bhûtas
Akhanda Japa *169*
  See also Japa
Akhanda Nâma Sankîrtana *169*
  See also Japa
Alabdha-bhûmikatwa *106*
Alasya *105*
Anâhata Chakra *125–126, 188*
Anavasthitatwa *106*
Anga-mejayatwa *114*
Animâ *119*
Antahkarana *133–134*
Antardhânam *121*
Anurmi-mattwam *120*
Ap *136*
  See also Mahâ-bhûtas

.

   (continued on next page)

Reviews

An important characteristic of the author is his ability to analyze a subject from all points of view, all possibilities, never having a partial unilateral vision. He always searches for the deepest and the most correct meaning. To have this broader and enlightened view from one of the most important ancient subjects of Indian Philosophy is a reward to everyone who will have the opportunity to read this book.

—Suzana de Albuquerque Paiva, Jungian Psychologist
Chief of the Department of Psychology at the Hospital Prontocor
Professor in the Faculty of Human Sciences
Fundação Mineira de Educação e Cultura
Belo Horizonte, Brasil

Swami Bhaskarananda has developed a good rapport with Western ideation; he has explained Patanjali in terms which can be easily understood and has done it well.

By helping to bring the wisdom of the East to the West the Swami provides a fertile basis for the genesis of ideas. This book should be of great interest to a very wide readership.

— Dr. David Longden, MA, MB,
B. Chir. (cantab.), DPM, FLCOM
Dorset, England